Christian Worship
in
Transition

CHRISTIAN WORSHIP IN TRANSITION

James F. White

Abingdon   Nashville

CHRISTIAN WORSHIP IN TRANSITION

Library of Congress Cataloging in Publication Data

WHITE, JAMES F
  Christian worship in transition.
  Includes index.
  1. Public worship. I. Title.
BV15.W46   264   76-16848

ISBN 0-687-07659-5

Scripture quotations are from the New English Bible, copyright © the Delegates of the Oxford University Press and the Syndics of the Cambridge University Press, 1961, 1970.

Chapter 3 contains materials that appeared in the author's article "Traditions of Protestant Worship" in *Worship*, May, 1975. Used by permission.

Chapter 4 contains material from the following: the author's article "Worship in Our Changing Culture" from *Worship: Good News in Action* © 1973, Augsburg Publishing House. Used by permission. The author's article "Worship and Culture: Mirror or Beacon?" in *Theological Studies* 35 (1974) 288-301; used by permission.

Chapter 8 comprises excerpts from *Liturgy* magazine © The Liturgical Conference, 1330 Massachusetts Avenue, N.W., Washington, D.C. 20005 1975. Used by permission of the copyright owner.

MANUFACTURED   BY   THE   PARTHENON   PRESS   AT
NASHVILLE, TENNESSEE, UNITED STATES OF AMERICA

Contents

To
Joseph D. Quillian, Jr.
friend, teacher, dean

Preface

Five years ago this week, just as 1970 passed into history, I found myself sitting before this same desk and typewriter, finishing the preface to *New Forms of Worship*. It was a heady time. Experimentation in worship had burst out everywhere; we were in the midst of exciting changes. Today much of that enthusiasm has disappeared, but the accomplishments and mistakes of that period live on. This book is written in a different atmosphere because we live in a different world. So it is a quite different book.

In both cases, my concern has been to record and evaluate what was currently happening in Christian worship. In 1970 it was still possible to attempt a comprehensive survey in systematic fashion of what was then current in worship. Today, things are even more amorphous, and I would not dare try a complete survey of the liturgical situation. Ten years after Vatican II, the revision and translation of the Roman Catholic liturgical books are still not quite complete, though the major work has been done. Ten years after experimentation became common in Protestantism, some have normalized it and others given up on it. Among both Catholics and Protestants the charismatic movement continues to grow. Yet it is hardly mentioned in these pages. Instead of a systematic survey, I have tried to write on areas that seem to me to be those of greatest present concern—our appropriation of history, worship and culture, and the meaning of the sacraments, to name a few. I hope I have chosen the areas of most widespread anxiety and that what I have to say on these topics will be of help to the perplexed.

Sometimes we get new direction by glancing back at the ground we have just covered. Much in these pages will reflect the way the terrain looked at the end of 1975. It is my hope that the view from this vantage may help us recollect where we have been during the past decade and help us map future directions. We have not come to this place by a direct route, but neither has it been a wandering in the wilderness. A sense of our present place and time may help us use the future more creatively.

I have tried hard to avoid repeating the materials covered in *New Forms*, though it has been tempting to make many of the same affirmations. Perhaps things have changed less than I anticipated they would when I wrote those pages in 1970; perhaps it is simply that I have changed my mind on fewer things than I had expected. In order to avoid repetition, a number of items are only roughed in here that are sketched out in detail in the previous book.

This book was originally conceived of as a collection of unconnected essays on worship. A few had been published in various periodicals, but I wanted a different audience for them. But, as the book developed and new material was added, coherence between the chapters grew. Ultimately the great majority of pages comprised material that I had not treated elsewhere. It is hard now to remember just which portions were written in rural seclusion in Vermont's Northeast Kingdom and which in Dallas' hectic activity.

Many of these pages were written during the pressures of various political and environmental campaigns when the phone never stopped ringing. (One of my friends says, "That's what liturgy will do for you!") I'm sure my prose would have been smoother if decisions had not had to be made between the paragraphs. But at least these involvements gave me a sense of relating to busy pastors whose sermons are always written under such conditions. I could not help being surprised how often consulting medieval sources and writing press releases blended in my days before the typewriter. This in itself may be a good mirror of the permanent and transient in worship.

It is always a pleasure to thank those who have contributed to a book. My only fear in this instance is that I might overlook some—they have been so numerous. Portions of this manuscript have been read by Professor Don E. Saliers, the Rev. Colbert S. Cartwright, the Rev. Hoyt L. Hickman, Rabbi Levi A. Olan, and my colleagues at Perkins School of Theology, Southern Methodist University: Professors H. Grady Hardin, Fred D. Gealy, Robert E. Elliott, David K. Switzer, James M. Ward, W. J. A. Power, William S. Babcock, and Roger Deschner. Their help has been enormous and has resulted in many improvements. Decherd H. Turner, Jr., Director of Bridwell Library, has been very generous in giving of his time and experience. I am indebted to my secretary, Yvonne Brown, for her skill and patience in deciphering my manuscript and producing fair copy at an amazing speed. My dean, Joseph D. Quillian, Jr., has given graciously of himself in reading and commenting on the entire manuscript just as he has supported my concern about Christian worship consistently for the past fifteen years. Last, I cannot fail to remember all the trips to town, all the ski sessions, all the evenings out, my wife, Marilyn, and our children, Lou, Bob, Ellen, Laura, and Martin, have foregone during past months in order that these pages could be brought to completion. I trust that this book completed is the most sincere Christmas present I can give them.

JAMES F. WHITE
Perkins School of Theology
Dallas, Texas

I

You Are Free—If

During the decade ending in 1975, I had the opportunity to do workshops in some three dozen states for people responsible for planning and leading services of Christian worship. I always found, when all was said and done, that I had just one thing to say: "You are free—if. You are free—if you know what is essential in any type of worship." The opposite of that is just as true. If you do not know what is essential in any type of worship, then you are completely captive.

"You are free—if." But that is a mighty big "if." I have found that many clergy and worship-commission members are not at all sure just what is essential as they plan for most types of worship. So they play it safe; they do it the way they have always done it. That may be the dullest and least imaginative way possible, but it involves no risks. We are, then, captive to the familiar unless we have a secure base camp from which to explore the unfamiliar.

This chapter is designed to help one think through just what is at stake in five basic types of Christian worship: the non-eucharistic Sunday morning service, the Lord's Supper, Christian initiation, weddings, and funerals. Except for sacred concerts, informal evening services, and prayer meetings, these five form the basic repertoire of most Protestant congregations. I shall try to define what is essential in each of these five types of services, especially what cannot be omitted.

I hope to challenge, in the process, some fixed assumptions by questioning some things we take for granted. That would be the first step to freedom. The second step is to use history and theology as basic tools in discerning the essentials in each type of service. Once we have taken these steps, we are free to follow the lead of our imagination. We may discover that some things we have clung to as security blankets are not important at all and others we have treated lightly may be bedrock. We shall also find that liberty, if we are to be responsible, has limits; there are things which we cannot dispense with. Knowledge of these limits will not limit our imagination but rather give it wide channels in which to flow.

What follows, then, is not intended to restrain us any more than the circular track limits the runner by keeping him where he can exert himself to the fullest advantage. Rather I want to say: "On your mark, get set, go!" My purpose is to encourage others to go as fast and as far as they can without wasting energy by wandering off the track. You are free if you have mastered the essentials by coming to know the nature and rules of the race set before you. We can paraphrase Augustine: "Know what you are doing and do as you please."

I

The most common service in Protestantism is the non-eucharistic Sunday morning service, which, curiously enough, has never received a name that is commonly accepted. Titles abound; it is called the Sunday service, morning order, morning prayer with sermon, service for the Lord's Day, divine worship, matins, service of the word, or just "the eleven o'clock." This babel of titles indicates a certain confusion as to both the form and purpose of this type of worship.

Our best way out of this maze is to use history to liberate us. The non-eucharistic Sunday morning service derives ultimately from the synagogue service. We are heirs of two and a half millennia of experience with this type of worship.

The synagogue service is basically a service of survival. What do you do in exile away from your own holy places and priests, your land and neighbors, in order not to lose all national identity? You remember your God and what he has done for your people. You "sing the Lord's song in a foreign land" (Ps. 137:4) by remembering. Survival, then, depends upon ability to remember God's actions.

The synagogue became, in effect, an exilic survival agency, and its worship became the prime means of keeping alive the corporate memories that were the foundation of the now defunct kingdom of Judah. It was possible to recall in worship what God had done for his people and to rejoice in these memories. Thus they could be passed on to future generations. Judah could survive through worship, though countless other conquered kingdoms perished completely. Worship could overcome even fire and sword.

It was found that writing down the memories was an important means of facilitating the recalling of God's actions. Teaching such writings through synagogue classes was useful. But the memories really came alive when they were read aloud, reflected upon, and rejoiced in by the gathered community. It is impossible to tell whether such an occasion at first was even considered worship, any more than the Pilgrims intended to establish a national thanksgiving festival in 1621. But worship it became as homesick Jewish exiles gathered for reading, reflecting, and rejoicing in what God had done for their ancestors. And every time they gathered to strengthen their common memories their identity was renewed.

The emphasis, though, was not on themselves but on what their God had done. They celebrated his actions not only in reading their history (scripture), but also in their songs (psalms), in their prayers of praise (blessing God for his acts), and in their reflections (sermons). In joyfully remembering their God, they discovered again and again who they themselves were. If God had acted so out of gracious mercy for their ancestors, surely his love remained with his people. In time, the reading of both law and prophets became standard so that they could recall how God gave himself in giving the law and in speaking to them through prophets.

Worship thus was a way of transmitting the corporate

memories of a people with whom God had covenanted. It was not the remembrance of a dead, detached past but a means of having God by worshiping him in the here and now. As past events were recalled, they became present reality through which God's saving powers were again and again experienced. Through worship, people could relive for themselves the whole history of salvation. Individual lives were changed by sharing in the recital of common memories, just as an adolescent is helped to discover his or her identity as the family together recalls past experiences by looking through their photograph album. Survival through identification with the group's corporate memories of how God had acted for his people is the core of synagogue worship.

The synagogue service still provides the basic form of the non-eucharistic Sunday service, and the content has changed only in the extension of the salvation history to its climax in the new covenant. Today we do the same things by the same means as exilic Jews: we recover our corporate history through scripture, song, prayer, and reflection. We rehearse together the events that make us a distinctive people.

Seventeenth-century England witnessed a remarkable debate between the Puritans, who believed that every form of worship had to be sanctioned by scripture, and the more conventional Anglicans, who argued that that was not necessary as long as nothing was done contrary to God's word. William Bradshaw, one of the Puritan leaders, argued "that whatsoever [is] done in . . . worship [that] cannot be justified by the said word [scripture], is unlawful."[1] Had not God himself told us through Moses: "See that you observe everything I command you: you must not add anything to it, nor take anything away from it" (Deut. 12:32). In case of doubt, the Puritans found plenty of other such texts: Deut.

---

[1] Quoted by Horton Davies in *The Worship of the English Puritans* (Westminster: Dacre Press, 1948), p. 50.

4:2, Josh. 1:7, Prov. 30:6, Matt. 15:9 ("their worship of me is in vain, for they teach as doctrines the commandments of men"), to mention a few. The Puritan argument was that only the forms that God had commanded could be used in worship.

Today, after a decade of experimentation in which there has been an abundance of forms of worship not ordained in scripture, the old Puritans vs. conventional Anglicans debate does not sound nearly as irrelevant as it once did. The Puritans would certainly have no difficulty today in discerning what was trivial, frivolous, or just celebration for celebration's sake. Simply check any form of worship to see if it can be justified by the word of God. If not, it is an offense to a "jealous God."

Before we dismiss this as mere legalistic biblicism, let us recognize that it is not nearly as wide of the mark as it might sound. Without doubt, the Puritans overstated their case in arguing that the actual *forms* of all worship depended upon biblical warrants. But they were dead right in insisting that the *contents* of worship depend upon the corporate memories of the community of faith as recorded in scripture. Had we listened to them in 1966, we would have heard a lot less in recent years about unqualified "celebration," a word now drained of meaning ("to honor"). We would have had fewer celebrations of life, a new day, joy, beauty, and a whole flock of other equally vague but high-sounding phrases. We would have had far more celebrations of the gospel, the good news, the Lord's Supper. Give me a "jealous God" any day rather than a reflection of our momentary feelings! Christian worship, as the Puritans realized, does have a biblical content, but once you realize that you are free from a rigid slavery as to its form. Christian worship can and ought to be biblical in content without being biblicist—i.e., restricting itself to forms prescribed in scripture.

Today we are free to devise our own forms for the Sunday service—free if we transmit the biblical memories. But the possible methods of transmission in this type of service are as free and varied as the horizons of our imaginations. The only requirement is that they work as well or better than conventional forms have for the *traditio, paradosis*, the giving over, the handing down, the passing on of that which we have received. It is the act of Paul: "for I received from the Lord what I also passed on to you" (I Cor. 11:23 literally). We received from scripture as the community's corporate memories what we also pass on by the most appropriate forms available in our time and place. If we can pass on the memories visually as well as verbally, if we can do it, say, through dramatizing the passion narratives rather than reading them, if we can sing the resurrection *exsultet* rather than preach it, why not?

The Sunday service is thoroughly biblical in content and could be called with good reason "the Bible service." But it is not biblicist in any narrowly legalistic way. It is biblical in content, not necessarily in form. Theologically the communications medium is largely neutral. Thus if pantomime can do better what rhetoric does, we are free to choose it. I do not believe that the memories of the Christian community can be communicated only by reading and preaching them, but whatever takes the place of these forms must do it equally well. Many a herald must have communicated his message long before he was within earshot. But his words were vital too. We are free to use the best available means or variety of means, conventional and novel, to recover the memories of God's dealings with his people.

But freedom always brings responsibility, and there are irresponsible acts that we are not free to commit. We are not free, for example, to substitute something else in place of the memories upon which the community's life together is based. I have preached in the country, and I know the relevancy of good roads. But a sermon on good roads has nothing to do with authentic remembrance in the body of Christ (despite Isa.

40:3). However relevant our message, if it is not devoted to the passing on of the gospel, it is out of place in the Sunday service.

A less obvious license, but equally damaging, is the indifference with which many services are structured. The congregation is almost challenged to find any connection between the reading of God's word, the praise of him for what has been read, and the exposition of it. All manner of items intrude between the reading of God's word and the preaching of it. Is it any wonder people are hard pressed to see any relation between lessons and sermon? The anthems, when not chosen as commentaries on the lessons, tend to become interludes of entertainment. I am not saying there is any ideal structure. If there is, I do not know it. But I am saying that we are not free to disregard how things function in worship. Clarity of function is obvious in the new Presbyterian *ordo* (structure) (*Worshipbook*, page 21) and in *Word and Table*, the new United Methodist publication. These facilitate the transmission of corporate memories rather than obscuring them.

There has been an attempt in recent years to make worship relevant by encouraging the articulation of the "concerns of the church," whereby people in the congregation spontaneously ask for prayer and service for specific individuals or groups. The purpose is commendable, the method sometimes questionable. We are not free to turn worship into a pep rally, no matter how splendid the cause. It is unfortunate when the concerns of the church degenerate into a recruitment period. That is a short-term, one-shot approach to relevance. The long-term approach offers these same concerns—where people are hurting and rejoicing—as prayers to God and offers our service to others as a sacrifice before him. The focus in worship should be not on what we do but upon God's doing, even though he may use us in the process. The Sunday service depends on what God does, past, present, and future.

II

The Lord's Supper (eucharist, holy communion, mass, divine liturgy, breaking of bread, Lord's memorial) is the other normal service on Sunday mornings, increasingly frequent in Protestant churches and invariably so in Roman Catholic churches. I shall discuss in the chapter following this one the theology of the Lord's Supper and the remaining services described here. Accordingly I shall be most brief in this chapter in dealing with meaning and concentrate on the rites themselves. The essence of the eucharist is that Christ acts in it to give himself to us anew as a gift. Just as any ordinary human giving of a gift conveys something of the giver himself or herself by renewing the relationship between two persons, so in the eucharist Christ acts to give himself to us as we are given bread and wine.

We act, too, in the Lord's Supper. It is through our gathering to give thanks (i.e., make eucharist) that Christ gives himself to us in this form of worship. We do it with all our senses and our whole body. The non-eucharistic Sunday service can become largely an intellectual affair, a "head trip," the eucharist never. For this reason, many have discovered in recent years that the Lord's Supper presents wide possibilities for experimentation. After all, it always has been what is now called multi-media. In theological terms, it is a sign-act through which new relationships are established or maintained by the use of actions and objects. We "do this," and the doing presents a variety of possibilities to spur on our imagination to liturgical creativity.

But we need pegs on which to hang our imagination. Fortunately, the Lord's Supper provides the necessary structure and yet leaves us free to apply our best creativity. Since the second century, and perhaps earlier, the Lord's Supper has had a definite shape, basically divided into two parts: the fore-mass or synaxis (the coming together) and the eucharist or communion (the union). The first of these consists essentially of the same ingredients as the Sunday service already described, so I shall not discuss it further. The second part consists basically of four acts both utilitarian in purpose yet highly significant in meaning (recalling the Last Supper): the *preparation* (take), the *giving thanks* (bless), the *fraction* (break), and the *distribution* (give). The last of these is the climactic sign of union with Christ and one another. Anything afterward is anticlimactic and brief. That is the basic structure, simple and solid, strong enough to support all manner of new ideas.

Of the four acts of the Lord's Supper, only one need detain us at this point. Many pastors tend to be intimidated by the second act (the giving thanks) so that they feel captive to the formularies provided by their denomination. The few who have ventured into original eucharistic prayers have often done so innocent of much knowledge of what they were doing, and the results have often proved so inadequate as to discourage further exploration of these possibilities. The material that follows is intended to give guidance and encouragement by showing the responsible way of using our liberty here.

There is a definite structure to the way Christians give thanks in the Lord's Supper. This structure is apparent in eucharistic prayers from the early third century right down to the present day. It appears in documents written before the canon of New Testament scriptures was finally determined and is at least as old as any creed. This very universality of the way Christians give thanks is a mirror of the community's perception of its relationship to God.

The eucharistic prayer is a hymn of praise and a creed of belief as much as a prayer. The Trinity forms its basis, though it is addressed throughout to God the Father. It begins in thanksgiving to God the Father, narrates the work of God the Christ, and invokes the Father to send God the Holy Spirit for our benefit. The concluding doxology, though addressed to God the Father, ties together the trinitarian nature of the whole prayer.

The eucharistic prayer opens with a *dialogue* of greeting between the celebrant and people and invites them to join in the giving of thanks, just as we might introduce grace before an ordinary meal. Then comes a joyful call to thanksgiving (the *preface*) in which often either a specific work of Christ is recited (varying according to season or occasion) or a general survey of salvation history is related. Until recently, Protestants have neglected both the variety possible in specific commemorations and the comprehensiveness of a full commemoration of God's actions beginning with creation. The thankful narration of God's acts is interrupted by a congregational acclamation of praise: "Holy, holy, holy" (the *Sanctus*) from Isa. 6:3 and Rev. 8:4 and "Blessed is he who comes in the name of the Lord" (the *Benedictus qui venit*) from Ps. 118:26 and Matt. 21:9. In the East, God's acts under the old covenant are usually recited before this acclamation, and the new covenant follows.

In the *post-Sanctus* the thankful narration resumes as we continue to recite God's works of salvation culminating in the *words of institution* as the events of the Last Supper are commemorated. Some traditions prefer to have the institution narrative elsewhere, but none neglects it. Many recent liturgies burst into a second congregational acclamation after the institution account with words such as "Christ has died,/Christ is risen,/Christ will come again."

Then occurs the remembering before God of what Christ has done (*anamnesis-offertory*) as we offer this memorial of his sacrifice. Usually this segment of the prayer refers concisely to Christ's death, resurrection, and ascension, offering these before God for our benefit.

Next comes an invocation, the *epiclesis*, in which God is asked to send the Holy Spirit upon the gifts and on the assembled congregation. The benefits desired from communion are detailed. Intercessions for the living and dead have sometimes occurred at this spot.

Triumphantly and joyfully all concludes with a trinitarian *doxology* and amen. The doxology sums up in praise the trinitarian theme of the whole prayer. Frequently the Lord's Prayer follows as a congregational act in which we address with familiar confidence the God who has done all these wonderful things simply as "Our Father."

All this sounds a lot more technical than it really is and doubtless prompts questions as to whether it is all necessary or simply a new form of legalism imposed on those who would give thanks as Christian people. Why is all this important? The way Christians give thanks reflects the very nature of Christianity in two ways. First, the eucharistic prayer is basically a creedal act. Indeed, for most of its history much of Western Christianity found any other creedal statement redundant at the Lord's Supper. Even today, a good eucharistic prayer makes a creed unnecessary, for such a prayer combines doxology and theology in a joyful statement of belief. Second, the eucharistic prayer represents the whole Jewish mentality of giving thanks by recital of what God has done, a mentality Christianity seems to have adopted without question. Thus the whole biblical mentality of think-thank forms the very basis for the eucharistic prayer. Every time we "do this" we thankfully show forth what God has done in Christ and testify to God's accessibility through recital of what he has done for us. It is a practice older than the written gospels and epistles and directly in line with Christ's use of the Passover occasion to combine re-enactment and presence in a new covenant.

When we know this, we are free to produce our own eucharistic prayers, fitting them to occasions and circumstances wherever we minister. The structure, given above, makes an infinite variety of possibilities available for making eucharist. All that is required is a knowledge of the basic structure and the imagination to word it for our own situations. Thus we can produce eucharistic prayers for weddings and funerals, for occasions of reconciliation and baptism, for Christmas and Pentecost. A good background is to study the denominational eucharistic prayers of the 1970s.

Indeed the whole Lord's Supper invites originality and innovation. We are free to find new ways of preparing, breaking, and giving the bread and wine if we can improve the sign value of those acts. Our freedoms in the service of the word have already been mentioned.

We have far more freedom in the Lord's Supper than any of us ever utilizes. But there are some things we are not free to do. We are not free to eliminate the service of the word with its proclamation of the memories which lie at the heart of the eucharistic community's life. We are not free to substitute something for bread and wine since nothing else can be identified with Christ's actions or represent in the same way his body and blood. Nor are we free to dispense with the fourfold actions, especially the great prayer of thanksgiving in which we recite God's actions of giving himself to us.

III

Our third major form of worship is at present undergoing major change in several traditions, so it is all the more important that we sort out the essentials in Christian initiation. Portions of this rite are often labeled by other names: baptism, confirmation, and first communion. I shall treat all portions under a single name, initiation, as more adequate. This has the advantage of showing the unity of the portions, and it avoids the unfortunate term "confirmation." Confirmation was the result of historic and geographic accidents and has been a practice looking for a theology ever since the term was first used early in the fifth century.

Accordingly, several traditions today are trying to eliminate the term, and some others have escaped its use entirely. I shall, instead, refer to this portion of the rite as laying-on-of-hands or sealing.

Initiation signifies the making of a Christian. Through it one enters into a new relationship to the body of Christ, the church. Initiation establishes a new relationship within the community of faith, and renewal of it is being seen increasingly as important in maintaining that relationship.

We will follow the new approach to initiation that seems to be in the process of development, especially among United Methodist, Lutheran, and Episcopal churches in this country. There seem to be two postulates to these developments: *Christian initiation ought to be complete at one time, and Christian initiation ought to be a lifelong process.* Behind this seeming contradiction lies a basic agreement. It is widely recognized that the forces that splintered initiation in early centuries in the West are irrelevant today and that the rationalizations of the middle ages and Reformation only compounded the problem. Initiation brings one fully into the community, not halfway. To baptize children and then to speak of them as only preparatory members and to deny them communion is to negate the whole function of baptism within the community's life. It is rather like being a member of a family but never being allowed to eat with it. Initiation is complete no matter at what age performed. It cannot be one thing for infants and another for adults. At whatever age one enters the community of faith the complete rite of initiation should be celebrated.

But we are also realizing that we do not remain the same but change and grow at every stage of life. We are the same person today and yet by no means the same as we were ten years ago or will be ten years hence. It has been found that occasional renewal of initiation can be a very helpful means of strengthening our Christian commitment. Recent years have seen a variety of services proposed: "Baptism, Confirmation, and Renewal" (United Methodist), "Affirmation of the Baptismal Covenant" (Inter-Lutheran Commission on Worship), and "Affirmation of Baptismal Vows" (Episcopal). Ultimately these reflect the yearly renewal of baptismal vows at the Easter vigil and may be used at such a time, at the Baptism of the Lord, the first Sunday in January, New Year's Eve, or on other occasions. On such a regular basis it can be a *general* renewal for the whole congregation. For others, as need arises, it can be a *special* affirmation of baptismal vows for those making this profession for the first time after due preparation and maturation, or those lapsed from Christian faith and practice who now return home, or those who have just experienced a climactic event in their religious life, or those new to a particular congregation or church body. It can combine these functions by singling out some people for special renewal or affirmation, and then all may join in a general renewal with such words as "Remember your baptism and be thankful."

What must one know to be free to innovate with initiation following this new and ancient approach? I shall describe the essentials under this method of unified initiation and lifelong renewal, but these can also be apportioned out to the fractured rite for those who find it necessary to follow a pattern with intervals of time between portions. Though we shall speak of these as separate acts, it is purely for convenience in describing them. I prefer to see all performed on the same occasion.

The first act, generally known as baptism, has four essential parts; the first three should not be dispensed with except for compelling reasons, and the fourth cannot be eliminated. The first is a series of questions scrutinizing the candidate's willingness to undergo conversion of life. This is usually answered with a *renunciation* of the temptations of this world.

A similar questioning tests conversion of belief, and the response takes the form of a *creedal affirmation*, trinitarian in shape and frequently following the form of the Apostles' Creed. Then follows a *prayer over the font*, which usually gives thanks by recalling the use of water in acts of salvation history from creation on, mentions Christ's commission to make disciples and baptize, and invokes the power of the Holy Spirit on the water and those to be baptized in it. The essential act, of course, is the *washing* with water and the use of the form of words baptizing each individual (by name) into the name of the Trinity.

Act two involves one or the other (or both) sign-acts which signify the transmission of power or the certification of such power. *Laying-on-of-hands* and *sealing* (anointing or chrismation) are acts, frequently mentioned in the New Testament, which call attention to the power of the Holy Spirit newly becoming manifest in those initiated into the community of the Spirit. Laying-on-of-hands is a dramatic act of conveyance of power or authority; sealing indicates an indelible mark of approval, an attestation or authentication, the mark of ownership and the owner's protection (Eph. 1:13 and 4:30), or the enduing with power (II Cor. 1:22).

Act three is the consummation of all that has preceded, the welcoming to the Lord's table for *communion* in the midst of the congregation. There are good arguments for performing baptisms in the context of the Lord's Supper so that those newly baptized and sealed might be allowed to participate for the first time in the community's most intimate gathering. This may present some difficulties with children, but I believe they should be allowed to partake regularly as soon as they can sit in church without disturbing too many people. The Lord's Supper is the portion of the initiation rite which is repeated constantly throughout our life, but the first partaking of it ought to be a significant occasion of welcome for new members of the body of Christ. Usually they would be the first of the congregation to receive communion.

Renewal comes at any age and is repeatable. Since this is a new development for most, the forms have quite a latitude. Usually they involve: a reaffirmation by everyone of the baptismal vows (both ethical and creedal), some form of prayer, perhaps the sprinkling of water toward everyone (using an evergreen branch and a basin of water or some other method), a laying-on-of-hands for those specially involved on this occasion, and communion for all.

At every act we are free to experiment if we understand the basic process. Other sign-acts may be added such as the traditional ones of giving the candle (illumination—Heb. 6:4 or Matt. 25:1-13), or a new garment (putting on Christ—Gal. 3:27), or ones freshly invented. It is possible to have the children of the congregation voice their prayers for a newly initiated baby. The results will almost certainly be both strange and wonderful. One can find other ways of showing forth this mystery.

We are not free to do certain things. Washing with water in the name of the Trinity is essential to baptism. The other acts just described are highly desirable, if not mandatory. We are not free to sentimentalize the process. The emphasis is not on the cuteness of babies but on what God does for them; and a rosebud, cooing, and kissing do not quite signify the action of the Almighty. We also are not free to initiate when there is little or no possibility of an infant being reared in the community where faith becomes a possibility. Promiscuous baptism is not one of our freedoms. Our freedom is shown in creative arrangement of the space where initiation takes place, the involvement of more of the congregation in the action, and the visual and audible aspects of washing. All these possibilities and many more demand the exercise of our imagination to signify more dramatically the happy event of the making of a Christian.

IV

The wedding service is a ceremony that ratifies a new relationship between two individuals through means of a public contract. In this service a visible and verbal event makes public record of this relationship in the midst of the worshiping community.

There are some special problems here, largely because of real uncertainty about whether the wedding service even belongs in the church. It existed outside the church for most of our history. By Chaucer's time it had come as far as the porch outside the church building, and by 1549 we finally got it inside. The church got into the act because it was necessary to have someone who could read and write (a *clerius*) in order to record the marriage for reasons of legitimacy and inheritance. For lack of other literates in medieval villages, the use of clergy became necessary. Today we sometimes wonder if it was worth the effort, since so many weddings become style or flower shows or society events. Would we be better off if all weddings took place outside the church? Sometimes I am tempted to think so, at least for couples who have no real Christian commitment.

But there have been many attempts in recent years to make the wedding service a fuller act of Christian worship than the older denominational services provide. Other innovations lend a contemporary spirit to the service. At the same time, there is a tendency, well recognized by liturgical scholars, that the greater the solemnity of an occasion the greater will be the desire to retain the most traditional possible forms. The former may be the desire of the couple themselves, the latter that of their parents. At any rate, many decisions have to be made, so it is important to sort out the essentials first.

To understand what is at stake in the wedding service, we must notice its curious fusion of both legal and religious significance. As already indicated, the service came into the church slowly, eventually reaching the church door where all legal contracts were ratified in the sight of God. The essence of the service even today remains a contract freely consented to before witnesses. The Council of Florence agreed that "the efficient cause of marriage is regularly the mutual consent uttered aloud on the spot."

The vows make a public contract before witnesses. "To have and to hold" are terms for the conveyance of property, the dating of said contract "from this day forward," the exclusion of any conditions "for better for worse," and the expiration "till death us do part"—all this is lawyers' talk, not liturgists'. Yet, ironically, the vows were the first part of the liturgy to appear in English, antedating the Reformation by a couple of centuries. Indeed, the whole marriage service was altered less by the Reformation than any other type of service.

In the vows a contract is freely entered into and publicly ratified before witnesses. It is a mutual and free consent, declares a lifelong intention, and excludes any conditions or reservations. The future husband and wife perform the vows; the clergy are there to preside but not to perform the service, although they often conduct it as if they did. It would be far better for the couple to face and speak to each other rather than, as is usually done, "facing the minister." Those gathered as witnesses are essential not only to prevent clandestineness and give legality but also to be a visible sign that the community of faith is welcoming a new family into its midst.

Beyond the vows and witnesses, we are free to innovate or regress. (I have even known a woman to insist on reinstituting the promise "obey him.") It is relatively easy, but a major advance, to add appropriate acts of worship from the Sunday service: lessons, psalms, prayers, a sermon, and hymns. Items involving congregational participation are especially important. The newest rites (Presbyterian, Lutheran, Episcopal, and United Church of Christ) provide these to greater or lesser degrees. New possibilities have appeared such as the congregation joining in a pledge "to support and uphold these two persons in their marriage" (Episcopal) or the whole congregation joining the couple in the recession with appropriate banners and placards. Most rites have been deficient in recognizing the gift of sexuality, though the 1972 Lutheran rite begins with the recognition that "God in his goodness created mankind [sic] male and female." Few modern rites even mention having children, though this is an important function of most marriages, but the new Episcopal rite recognizes it in several optional prayers. Such mention is all the more relevant when children from a previous marriage are present and ought to be recognized as part of a new unit.

Perhaps we might do well to provide a wedding service performed in the church building but without any specific Christian references. This would free us to make wedding celebrations for those within the Christian community more definitely an act of worship. For those outside the community, we would cease to pretend but simply provide a public service. It is ironic that it took us so long to get the wedding into the church, and now we cannot get some of them out.

There are some things about the Christian wedding that we are not free to remove. One of these is the public exchange of vows before witnesses, vows that pledge lifelong commitment without any qualifications. Obviously we are not free to preside over the marriage of those who do not have a valid wedding license from the state. Likewise, we are not free to preside over the marriage of those whom our church does not allow to be married. The various churches do have rules about who may be initiated, ordained, and married. We do not serve people well or gain the respect of the public by compromising our own standards. T. S. Eliot reminded us that there are times when the church is tender when we wish she were hard, and hard when we wish she were soft.

V

Christian burial signifies the transition to another stage of existence within the body of Christ. One departs this life but not the community of faith. Instead, the church gathers to mark the passage into a new relationship of the faithful departed as he or she is born into eternity instead of into time. It was a transition greeted with hope in the early church, shrouded in fear in the middle ages, and quietly ignored as far as possible by the modern church. We have ended up being far more superstitious about death than our medieval ancestors were as we cherish illusions that death is only sleep, that the body can be preserved instead of being a part of nature, and the name kept unforgotten forever.

There are two purposes served by Christian burial in addition to the utilitarian act of disposing of the body in a sanitary fashion. The first of these is the consolation of the bereaved. The funeral functions as part of the necessary grief therapy. I would like to suggest two ways this process is aided by Christian burial: by a biblical realism about death and by a witness to our trust in God.

The Bible makes no mistake about the reality of death. "We shall all die; we shall be like water that is spilt on the ground and lost" (II Sam. 14:14). A religion at whose center is the cross, emblem of suffering and death, can hardly evade the reality of death. Mortality is a basic condition of being human and is part of God's plan for humanity. We really do people little service by hiding the reality of death and the physical separation it brings by using euphemisms about passage, sleep, crossing the bar, or whatever. These can be misused to avoid the reality of death and thus prolong the grief experience. The funeral testifies to the reality of death but does so in the midst of a supporting community.

The last word, though, is not about death. Indeed, we know so little about death other than its reality that we have to approach the subject with a reverent agnosticism. But what we do know, what matters above all else is the trustworthiness of God. So the funeral stresses that "there is nothing in death or life . . . nothing in all creation that can separate us from the love of God in Christ Jesus our Lord" (Rom. 8:38-39). The last word is "God," who does not forsake us even at the time of death. Thus most services of Christian burial are comprised largely of the words of scripture, which are far stronger in promise than any other poetry or prose. These passages ought to be read (not recited) directly from the Bible so that the strong sense of proclaiming God's word from scripture itself is communicated. At this point, God's word and only God's word really matters. The sermon, though it ought to underscore the real and unique individuality of the deceased, should also affirm that even in death God remains worthy of our absolute trust.

The service of Christian burial serves, first of all, to console the bereaved. For the burial of a Christian, this would seem to be best accomplished through appropriate lessons from the Old Testament, epistles, and Gospels, and especially items involving congregational participation such as psalms, hymns, and a creed. Christian burial has a second function, too, that of commending the deceased to God. Of course, this too is directly related to consolation of the bereaved, but Protestants have been very anxious over this act for fear it implies a concept of purgatory. So we go against our very nature; we pray for a person to the moment of death and then we cease to pray. Surely this runs contrary to human instincts. Surely we can invoke for them "entrance into the land of light and joy, in the fellowship of thy saints" (Episcopal) without worrying about presuming to know more about death than we can. And most naturally we can give thanks to God for the life that has been given and recognize in it "a source of renewed fellowship with all the saints" (Methodist).

The burial of the dead or "Witness to the Resurrection"

(Presbyterian) is one of the most free-form services in most service books. Yet we are free to add much that is not even suggested there. More reference to baptism, in which one has already potentially died and risen with Christ, is a possibility. During the church service, why not cover the coffin with a pall on which are symbols of our trust in God? In some Christian communities a celebration of the eucharist is most appropriate as a testimonial to the fellowship of the church on both sides of death. There are great possibilities musically. Perhaps someday, as in the early church, Christian burial can again be the triumphant procession of the victorious soldier now safely home.

There seem to be few limits to our freedom here. These limitations would seem only to be at forms that try to disguise the reality of death or fail to witness to the trustworthiness of God. Except for these restrictions and anything contrary to concern for the bereaved, we are free indeed.

When all has been said, it is surprising how few are the restraints on the different types of Christian worship and how wide are the possibilities. In all these services we have extraordinary latitude as long as we are sure what is essential. Our liberty is in Christ, who has set us free. It is up to us to use this freedom creatively and responsibly. You are free—if you know what you are doing and why.

II

Basics of
Sacramental Theology

There are two sharply contrasting approaches to the sacraments in American Protestantism today. Both approaches are widely found; neither is limited by the boundaries of denominations or the different Protestant traditions. They exist side by side in almost any congregation whatever the denomination. I name these approaches for their historical sources, calling one "Enlightenment" and the other "traditional." I shall explain these terms and then attempt a brief contemporary statement of sacramental theology.

The *Enlightenment* view of the sacraments regards them as human actions to help us remember God's actions. This is probably the prevalent view among American Protestants, even in traditions that originated prior to the Enlightenment of the eighteenth century or in reaction to it.

In this approach, the role of humans is all important. Not only do we perform the sacraments ourselves but their power seems to depend entirely upon our ability to use these actions to remember God and what he has done in the past. Thus the sacraments are human actions to stimulate human memories of divine actions from biblical times. They become stimulants of sentiment. All this is usually linked to ethical consequences. Remembrance of God's past action is looked upon as a strong incentive for leading a better life in the future and for helping others do likewise.

This whole approach has fundamental consequences for the sacramental life of many Protestants. If the sacraments depend upon human activity, then they have often been seen as needing considerable human preparation, particularly of an introspective nature. This might take the form of communal self-examination in the week-long preparations for the sacrament Sunday by congregations in the Scottish highlands or the fervent confessions of individuals savingly wrought upon in American frontier campmeetings. However commendable such pitches of fervor might be, they could not long be sustained. For a variety of groups, the Lord's Supper became an occasional affair, celebrated only after periods of preparation for which it became the capstone. With the exception of the Christian Church (Disciples of Christ), most congregations in which an Enlightenment view of the sacraments prevails have not had frequent communion services.

Of course, in time, the disciplined self-examination tended to decay, but by then the pattern of infrequent communion services had prevailed. For many people this sacrament became increasingly meaningless. If all depends on our ability to remember God and we are not disciplined to prepare for this climactic event, then it is not surprising that for many people it becomes increasingly a disappointing occasion. Many churches have noted a drop in attendance on communion Sundays apparently because people feel they "get less out of it." What has happened, in effect, is that the human activity has not been sufficient to make us experience the remembrance of God with any fervor. With the decay of our disposition to remember came a general decline in the sacramental life.

The term "Enlightenment" has been chosen as an appropriate label for this approach to the sacraments, but it needs some modification historically. This is particularly true in the case of baptism, where a marked shift had developed early in the Reformation. In the writings of the Zurich Reformer, Ulrich Zwingli, the sense of baptism as a divine act with inherent sacramental efficacy gets pushed aside for a concept of baptism as dedication and pledge of what humanity ought to do. In 1525 Zwingli wrote his treatise *Of Baptism* against the Anabaptists in order to refute their denial of infant baptism. But his defense of infant baptism subjected it to a radical change in meaning from that of Catholic Christianity and Luther.

Zwingli found that Matt. 28:19 meant "With this external sign you are to dedicate and pledge them to the name of the Father, the Son and the Holy Ghost, and to teach them to observe all the things that I have committed to you."[1] He goes on to say "that baptism is simply a mark or pledge by which those who receive it are dedicated to God."[2] Baptism as dedication first comes to the fore, as far as I can tell, in Zwingli's writing.

Characteristic is his statement that "the external baptism of water cannot effect spiritual cleansing. Hence water-baptism is nothing but an external ceremony. . . . It is clear and indisputable that no external element or action can purify the soul."[3] Indeed, in rejecting the traditional concepts of baptismal efficacy, Zwingli even out-spiritualized the Anabaptists, chiding them for setting "too great store by the baptism of water." In place of the medieval sense of baptism as signifying and conferring grace, we find, in Zwingli, that baptism becomes an intellectual and ethical pledge of our obligations to God rather than a witness to God's action.

The consequences of such a radical departure took time to develop. One can see the process at work in the disappearance of the prayer over the font (the flood prayer) in such baptismal rites as the Methodist. This prayer (based on I Pet. 3:20-21) proved too much for the Enlightenment mentality of nineteenth-century American Methodists, and they discarded what Wesley had retained. The 1964 Methodist baptismal rite bore no trace of this central prayer in the baptismal rite for children, though it has finally returned full grown in the 1976 alternative service. Zwingli's views had triumphed, aided and

---

[1] *Zwingli and Bullinger*, G. W. Bromiley, ed. (Philadelphia: Westminster Press, 1963), pp. 145-46.
[2] *Ibid.*, p. 146.
[3] *Ibid.*, p. 156.

abetted by the Enlightenment, which was scandalized as much as he by the very thought of external actions being able to purify the soul.

Thus infant baptism came to be considered by many parents a dedication of infants and is even called such by some church people. Explicit in this is the assumption that baptism is something that parents do for their children in pledging to rear them in the faith. Not only does this reduce baptism to a purely human activity but it eliminates all the biblical images of baptism for an entirely nonbiblical one—dedication based on human action, not on God's.

A similar aspect operated with the baptism of adults. Zwingli spoke of baptism as a pledge and dedication which committed them to discipleship. This act marked "wandering sheep" for God and brought them to the "true shepherd." In this sense, baptism is an "initiatory sign or pledge with which we bind ourselves to God."[4] It resembles something of a high-level form of religious education, and this seems to be the sense in which Barth interpreted baptism in recommending it only for adults."[5] In popular practice, believers' baptism often seems to be a self-commitment in which adults pledge and dedicate themselves to a life of faith and piety. At its worst, it can be conceived of as a reward for having such attributes.

There is not a great deal of difference between baptism of infants and believers' baptism when both are seen solely as actions humans perform in pledging or dedicating either one's child or oneself. In either case, baptism is treated as a human act helping us to be mindful of God. Many of those who do practice infant baptism have a deeper affinity than they may realize with many of those who practice only believers' baptism. Both have departed radically from the traditional

---

[4]*Ibid.*, p. 148.

[5]*The Teaching of the Church Regarding Baptism* (London: SCM Press, 1959).

Christian understanding of baptism. Unfortunately antagonisms between pedobaptists (those who baptize infants) and antipedobaptists frequently conceal from large numbers of both that, differ though they may as to who are fit candidates for baptism, they share the same Enlightenment approach to what happens in this sacrament. It is a view that pervades a large segment of American Protestantism.

The Lord's Supper provides another instance of the same Enlightenment approach. For many Protestants, the Lord's Supper is basically a commemorative event stimulating our reflection on the death and resurrection of Jesus and provoking us to greater moral earnestness. One of two phrases are carved on many communion tables or sewn on altar frontals in America: "In remembrance of me" or "Holy, Holy, Holy." These two unconsciously sum up the Enlightenment and the traditional approaches to this sacrament. For the former, the Lord's Supper is a memorial meal, helping us to remember what Jesus did in his passion, death, and resurrection. But the vision of his present action, implied in "Holy, Holy, Holy," remains unstated in many churches.

The thoughts of many, if not most, American Protestants about the Lord's Supper were well stated by Bishop Benjamin Hoadly, 1676–1761, a prominent Anglican bishop. In his *Plain Account of the Nature and End of the Sacrament of the Lord's-Supper*, Bishop Hoadly spoke of eating and drinking: "in remembrance of Christ; and this to be continued, until He, who was once present with his disciples, and is now absent, shall come again."[6] Bishop Hoadly felt people were being deterred from partaking of the sacrament by a too serious consideration of their unworthiness. Accordingly, he minimizes the preparation necessary. He is, rather, concerned with the practical consequences of fulfilling this "duty":

---

[6] (London, 1735), p. 24. Capitalization and italics modernized.

The benefits received, from all such performances, by reasonable creatures, cannot possibly be received but in a reasonable way. These duties, how well soever performed, cannot be supposed to operate as charms; nor to influence us, as if we were only-clockwork, or machines, to be acted upon by the arbitrary force of a superior being. . . . By our partaking of the Lord's Supper . . . we profess ourselves Christ's disciples; and acknowledge our obligation to live according to his laws. . . . This is therefore, an effectual acknowledgment of our strict obligation to all instances of piety, and virtue. . . .

And what reasonable creature would not be content with benefits of this sort, which are always of substantial and lasting service; without fancying to himself privileges, communications, or impressions from above, of another sort, never expressly promised to this duty. . . .

If any persons think this is a low character of such a rite, . . . this must arise either from the low opinion they have conceived of the highest good of mortal man; which is the uniform practice of morality, . . . or, from the notion they have entertained of some express promise annexed by God to this duty . . . [i.e.] fond and groundless imaginations of things never included in this rite by its great and good founder.[7]

Modernize the language a bit, and you have essentially the eucharistic doctrine of many of our contemporaries: recollection of Jesus' death helps us lead better lives. In the case of the Lord's Supper, Bishop Hoadly comes closer to being their spokesman than Zwingli, for whom there was a much stronger sense of the spiritual presence of Christ in the community gathered in his name. For Zwingli, as Bard Thompson has said, the eucharist "was anything but a bare memorial" to believers, but rather affirmed "contemplation, fellowship, thanksgiving, and moral earnestness."[8]

In Enlightenment Protestantism, then, the Lord's Supper was basically a means of fixing our attention on Jesus Christ, especially on his death so that we might live sacrificially too.

---

[7]*Ibid.*, pp. 154-57.
[8]*Liturgies of the Western Church* (Cleveland: World, 1961), p. 146.

Sober reenactments of the Last Supper stressed the sorrowful aspects and provoked genuine moral earnestness. The thrust seemed to be: "If he, . . . can't you at least?"—a Gethsemane piety. But ultimately, all here depended upon the worshipers' ability to remember Jesus.

At the heart of this Enlightenment approach to the sacraments is a basic distrust of the use of the physical in the spiritual endeavors of humanity. It often seems implied that the chief reason for observing the sacraments is that we are stuck with them on the basis of scripture. But two is enough and, thank heaven, only two seem to rest on divine command! A biblical literalism has kept the two sacraments alive as "duties" even when the Enlightenment seemed to resent them. It did its best to strip them of mystery and to make them straightforward exercises in remembering the Lord God and stimulating us to obey his moral laws.

By contrast, the *traditional* approach to the sacraments asserts that God is the chief actor in the sacraments and that humans are the recipients of what God does through the sacraments for us and our salvation. Consistently the emphasis is on what God does for us. This is usually expressed in terms of grace, i.e., "the supernatural assistance of God." A typical statement is that "our sacraments both contain grace and confer it upon all who receive them worthily."[9] Bernard Leeming insists: "Grace is the intimate personal relationship between God and man, which changes not only man's thoughts *but his being.*"[10] God changes our being through the operation of his grace in the sacraments.

Protestants expressed the same basic conception. Luther saw the sacraments as ways in which God acts to give us the

---

[9] Pope Eugenius IV, "An Account of the Seven Sacraments" (1438), in Ray C. Petry, *A History of Christianity* (Englewood Cliffs, N.J.: Prentice-Hall, 1962), p. 324.

[10] *Principles of Sacramental Theology* (London: Longmans, 1963), p. 3. Italics mine.

benefits he has promised us in scripture. Though he could not find sufficient biblical warrant for the same number of sacraments as the Catholics, Luther was no less firm in asserting God's action through them. Calvin, too, asserted the power of God in the sacraments by which he grafted us into his body and raised us to feed upon Christ. The Church of England's Articles of Religion say: "Sacraments ordained of Christ be . . . effectual signs of grace, and God's good will towards us, by the which he doth work invisibly in us." John Wesley spoke of baptism and the Lord's Supper as "means of grace" through which the power of God operates.

These Protestant theologians assert as clearly as their Catholic counterparts that God is the chief actor in baptism and the Lord's Supper and that humans are the recipients of what God does. Thus the traditional approach has a high Protestant ancestry as well as Catholic.

Another way of labeling this view is to call it a "supernatural" approach. It does not try to avoid the assertion that God uses the physical objects and actions of this world to accomplish his will for us here and now. Those who hold this view see it as consistent with the way the community of faith has experienced God's actions as recorded in scripture. It also means that the efficacy of the sacraments does not depend entirely on us and on our ability to think about God or to lead holy lives. Indeed, there is a liberating quality in this approach in that we are freed from the necessity of making the sacrament happen. For this view says it is not our ability to imagine the Savior in the upper room or on the cross that ultimately matters, not our staunch resolution to lead a holier life that finally counts, not the fervor of our devotion that is crucial, but simply the trust that God works here to accomplish his purposes in his way.

Now this cannot be carried so far as to say humans have no responsibility here. Both Catholics and Protestants stress the need of an appropriate disposition on the part of the recipient.

We can oppose obstacles, we can resist grace, we can be without faith or sorrow for sin. Our participation in responsible fashion, then, is necessary in order actually to receive God's gifts. But God's work here does not depend upon our worthiness or our ability to think on spiritual things. God acts and we receive or we can refuse. But according to the traditional approach, all ultimately depends on God's action in the sacraments, not on our devotion or resolution, though his action can change both.

I expect many will recognize that there are various possible combinations of these views I have called "Enlightenment" and "traditional." Obviously, I have oversimplified for sake of brevity, but I hope I have shown two fundamentally different approaches to sacramental theology as the chief current options in American Protestantism.

It is probably evident by this point that, of the two possibilities, the traditional view of the sacraments is the one I prefer, though in some untraditional ways. I realize this is not the approach familiar to many American Protestants including recent generations of my own tradition. To some it will seem a regression to a past which they think we outgrew more than two centuries ago, a return to irrational and murky theological darkness.

I would reply that there are three good reasons for preferring the traditional approach to the Enlightenment one, even though the latter is more familiar. First, I conceive the traditional view to be much closer to the whole biblical narrative of a God who acts in history using objects (a burning bush, a quaking mountain) and actions (smashing a clay pot, making a yoke) to accomplish his will. In the same vein, the Bible presents God as acting to forgive sins in baptism (Acts 2:38) or to give his Holy Spirit through laying-on-of-hands (Acts 8:17). Many American Christians have a deep reverence for the words of scripture but see the sacraments through Enlightenment glasses. Yet the Enlightenment is scandalized by assertions that God acts in our time through the sacraments just as he does throughout scripture. The traditional view seems more faithful, then, to the biblical witness.

Second, I have indicated, the traditional view is that of Catholic history and a majority of the great Protestant reformers and historic confessions. There are some significant exceptions such as Zwingli on baptism, some of the Anabaptists, and Protestant representatives of the Enlightenment. The contemporary eclipse of the traditional approach to sacramental theology is not the only area in which the popular piety of our times has drifted far from the moorings of the reformers. Original sin is a concept also repugnant to Enlightenment mentality but basic to Luther, Calvin, and Wesley.

The third reason is the one that concerns me most. An important argument for the traditional view today is that it is in tune with what we are learning about how to experience our full humanness. More and more we realize how our lives are shaped and how we shape the lives of others through the use of sign-acts. The sacraments reflect this profoundly human experience. This is how we are. Calvin said it best when he noted that God "so tempers himself to our capacity that . . . he condescends to lead us to himself by these earthly elements, and to set before us in the flesh a mirror of spiritual blessings. . . . He imparts spiritual things under visible ones . . . marked with this signification by God."[11] The Creator knows his creatures best. We give ourselves to others through sign-acts; God does no less.

The traditional approach to the sacraments, it seems to me, is more faithful to the Bible, has a longer history, and comes closer to expressing our full humanness. Accordingly, I shall develop this approach in the remainder of this chapter. I want to state in contemporary terms the traditional view that God

[11] *Institutes of the Christian Religion* IV, 14, 3 (Philadelphia: Westminster Press, 1960), II, 1278.

acts in the sacraments. I shall examine this in the sacraments treated together first, then individually.

I

I have said scripture speaks of God as acting in the sacraments. We need to look at this in light of the nature of God. Central in the whole Christian concept of the deity is that God gives himself to us. We do not worship a complacent deity who stands aside to admire his creation and never interferes in its running. Both testaments are records of God's interventions in which he enters history to give himself to his people.

The Old Testament is largely narrative of how God enters history to effect his will. He gave himself to his people by delivering them from captivity, by making covenant to be their God and king, by giving them laws, by settling them in a land flowing with milk and honey. He gave himself by providing kings and speaking to his people through prophets. And he gave himself during their captivity and return from exile.

The New Testament climaxes the story with God's giving of himself in the incarnation. God became the man, Jesus, and "made himself nothing, assuming the nature of a slave" (Phil. 2:7). The Apostles' Creed sums up God's self-giving in Jesus Christ as the supreme act of giving. His giving does not end with the New Testament events but goes on to judgment when time ends.

In all this recital, it is important to recognize that it is God, and only God, who determines how he will give himself. Invariably his actions come as surprises to humanity. We do not dictate the terms. Nothing could be more unexpected than God "assuming the nature of a slave." Nothing could be more surprising than his choice of a small nation of Hebrews as his chosen people. God upsets all our notions of wisdom; "God has made the wisdom of this world look foolish" (I Cor. 1:20).

He takes the initiative in determining how he will give himself to us. Almost always it strikes the world as paradox:

> He has brought down monarchs from their thrones,
>   but the humble have been lifted high.
> The hungry he has satisfied with good things,
>   the rich sent empty away. (Luke 1:52-53)

This is not the way the world gives. But God alone determines how, when, and to whom he chooses to give himself.

There is, however, one constant in God's giving of himself to us. His self-giving is experienced most consistently in and through the life of a community. This resounds throughout the Old Testament where God gives himself to his people through a concrete event. The people then continue to experience this self-giving by commemorating it through reenactment. Certain events became keys to all events, and God is experienced through reliving these crucial events. Even in exile his people recall who they are by reciting the history of God's key acts of self-giving to them as a people. In time, these corporate memories of God's giving became the community's book, the scriptures.

The same applies to the new Israel, the church. As such, we know God as one who became flesh in order to give himself for us. We know God's gifts because they are recalled for us as the scriptures are read in worship week after week. We know his actions as they become present through preaching. For preaching is a fresh event through which God gives himself to us again and again. As the community listens for God's word, he acts to give himself to us in our here and now. It is a word heard not in isolation but in the community gathered for the reading and preaching of God's word.

The reading of scripture and preaching depend not just on humanity but on God's action. The power of preaching is from God, but is is experienced in community. We gather to hear God's word as he gives himself afresh to the community of faith. Thus preaching, too, is far more than simply a way in which we refresh our memory of God, for it is a new event in which he reaches out to us as giver. Preaching, then, is not completely contingent upon our action for its efficacy, though we can place an obstacle in its way.

Likewise, the Christian assembly experiences God as giver through sharing in the sacraments. The sacraments, like preaching, are social acts, usually performed in community and always relating to the community. Thus a private baptism, though valid, is clouded and untrue to its nature in that it does not help members of the community recall their own baptism, nor does it present them an opportunity to commit themselves to the nurture of the new member of the body. Private confession was the result of drastic change from primitive practices, and once again the sacrament of reconciliation is being celebrated as a public act. Private ordination would be a travesty. Even anointing the sick would seem to carry its highest sign value when representatives of the total community are present (James 5:14-16).

The sacraments are social acts in which God relates to the Christian community and members of it relate to God and to one another by acquiring new roles or in recovering old roles. Thus each sacrament has at its heart relationships between individuals, between individuals and community, and between individuals and God in community. The variety of sacraments reflects various types and occasions of these differing relationships. The sacraments form a network of relationships among individuals, community, and God.

These relationships have one common characteristic: they are relationships of love within community. In the sacraments it is signified to us that each of these relationships is a relationship of love appropriate to the circumstances and persons involved. Our celebration of the sacraments gives us power to help perfect the appropriate form of love.

Some illustrations of these differing relationships of love

may be helpful. In matrimony two persons are united in a particular relationship of love supported by the love for both of the whole community. In another form of love, reconciliation reunites a community in which we have wounded one another by sin. Through the love of God, we are forgiven and joined to one another. Baptism incorporates us into God's family, where, as members of one another, we become the objects of one another's loving concern. In each instance the form of love varies—conjugal, reconciling, or adoptive—but the functions of the sacraments are similar: making love visible and helping perfect it. *Our first principle, then, is that the sacraments are communal events involving relationships of love.*

It is characteristic of human love to need visible signs. Indeed, human relationships of all types depend upon visible signs and sign-acts. Our very bodies are signs to others of our relationships to them. As Schillebeeckx says, "The human body does not refer to a soul situated *behind* it, it is not a *sign* of the spirit: it is, on the contrary, this interiority itself made visible."[12] This "interiority itself made visible" through our physical body communicates in all types of human relationships. Thus the sign is not something distinct from the reality of these relationships but a part of that reality. It helps build up and supports those relationships itself. In this sense, the sign has a reality of its own.

Our relationships depend on signs. "The relationship between people comes into being in signs, and through signs it is further developed."[13] The kiss is a good example: "The kiss is love itself, embodied in a sign."[14] Signs, of course, can be dissimulations—Judas kissed Jesus—but usually they are used with genuineness to embody an actual relationship. Yperman

---

[12] Edward Schillebeeckx, O.P., *The Eucharist* (New York: Sheed & Ward, 1968), p. 100.

[13] Joseph Yperman, *Teaching the Eucharist* (New York: Paulist Press, 1968), p. 10.

[14] *Ibid.*, p. 11.

says it well: "Only through signs do we come to exist with and for one another. The relationship, in its search for signs, is searching for itself. No love exists that assumes no signs."[15]

We need signs to relate to one another simply to be human. But human relationships are not static. They change and develop, decay or vanish. Relationships need renewing to be kept intact. Signs help create new relationships and renew old ones. It is hard to imagine love that does not involve some such visible form as the sign-acts of giving a gift or doing a favor. A relationship of hate, likewise, would be embodied in its own perverse sign-acts of discourtesy. Various acts—giving, kissing, slapping—create new realities or sustain old ones as we relate to one another. We cannot live without them, especially signs of love. Indeed, signs of love, such as the kiss, often become synonymous with love itself. Love needs these visible signs in order to develop and grow.

It should not surprise us, then, that the sacraments deal with relationships of love by giving visibility to love through various sign-acts. Traditionally it has been common to say that three things are necessary for the sacraments: objects or "material," words or "form," and the person of the "ministrant," who acts with the intention of performing what the church does. In briefer terms, we can speak of these as constituting sign-acts. A sacramental sign-act encompasses a person's saying words and using objects. It is, in short, both visible and audible. The sacraments are sign-acts that show forth love.

But the sacraments are sign-acts that operate within a special community. Thus they have a distinctiveness from other sign-acts. They are based on the memories and hopes of the community of faith. And so they are shaped by the ways the Christian community understands its very being. They help us perceive and express love in Christian terms as those

---

[15] *Ibid.*, p. 12.

who know ourselves dependent upon God's love. We cannot simply assume that sign-acts that signify love in ordinary life are adequate substitutes for sacraments. Such secular sign-acts lack the shared history, the memories, that unite the Christian community. *Our second principle is that sacraments are sign-acts that make love visible within the community of faith.*

At the very heart of the sacraments is God's supreme disclosure in making his love for us visible in Jesus Christ. In Jesus Christ "we saw his glory" (John 1:14). The Word came to dwell among us and make the Father known. In Jesus Christ we see what humanity never saw before, the glory of God visible in human flesh. Here we see the true nature of God's love, made visible before our eyes.

Love is visible in Jesus Christ not just in what he said and did but in his whole being, in his giving himself for us, in his making "himself nothing, assuming the nature of a slave. . . . He humbled himself, and in obedience accepted even death— death on a cross" (Phil. 2:7-8). Thus his whole being was a visible sign-act. Schillebeeckx entitled the most important book on sacramental theology of the last two decades *Christ the Sacrament of the Encounter with God.* He says: "The man Jesus, as the personal visible realization of the divine grace of redemption, is *the* sacrament, the primordial sacrament."[16] In Christ's self-giving for us we find in "historical visibility" the manifestations of God, the true epiphany.

In the fifth century, Leo the Great said in an Ascension Day sermon, "What was visible of our Redeemer has now passed over into the sacraments."[17] Jesus Christ took mortal flesh, which could not last forever on earth. But in the sacraments he takes visible forms which can show forth his love until he

---

[16](New York: Sheed & Ward, 1963), p. 15.

[17]Sermon LXXIV, *Sources Chrétiennes* (Paris: Editions du Cerf, 1961), LXXIV, 140.

comes again. What matters for our salvation is given us in the sacraments that we might experience anew his love. The sacraments are a means of proclaiming his love until he appears again. In the sacraments Christ continues till the end of time to show forth the nature of divine love just as he did during his years of "historical visibility" among us.

The sacraments can be called an extension of the incarnation, for Christ continues to work in them throughout time and space. Paul calls the church which celebrates the sacraments "Christ's body" (I Cor. 12:27). In this community of faith, Christ's work continues whenever his people gather for worship and his love again acquires visible signs through the sacraments. Another way of saying this is that God gives himself to us through the sacraments just as he has given himself to us through his actions in the past, especially in the Christ event.

I prefer to speak of God as giving himself to us rather than to follow convention in speaking of this act as grace. I am not denying that the sacraments contain and confer grace. I am stating, rather, that the use of the human analogy of self-giving seems easier to grasp than grace, which has no immediate human counterpart. Furthermore, it seems better to speak of this self-giving as direct action between God and humanity rather than to introduce a third entity—grace—to this relationship. I am concerned to speak of what happens in the sacraments as dynamic action rather than as a static category, as grace sometimes seems to appear in theological discussions. God gives himself to us in the sacraments just as we give ourselves to others by various sign-acts. Only he has so much more to give: abiding mercy, gracious promise, saving will, purposeful love, etc. *Our third principle, then, is that the sacraments are a direct and personal self-giving of God to us.*

God gives himself to us in relationships of love simply because his very nature is love. First John says it most simply: "For God is love" (4:9). And because he is love, his gift of himself to us enables us to become more perfect in our love for one another. By his love he makes us a new people; as a people of love we are able to serve him and one another. The community of faith is also the community of love, and its service of all humanity flows from the love it has received. In all this the love of God is prior. He gives himself to us so we can give ourselves for others.

God gives himself to us in two ways in the sacraments: his love helps establish new relationships of love within the Christian community and it also maintains old relationships of love. Obviously these are not completely separate categories. But there is a difference between baptism, where we are initiated into the body of Christ, and communion, whereby we are nourished in that body throughout our lives. There are parallels in ordinary human relationships such as the sign-act of an initial handshake or the lifetime of correspondence that may ensue. Establishment and maintenance of relationships are even more obvious in the life of a community where members play differing roles. Each of these roles begins at some point in time and is sustained thereafter. *Our fourth principle is that God gives himself to us in the sacraments through establishing and maintaining relationships of love.*

There has been much controversy in recent centuries over the number of the sacraments. This is a tragic irony, for during most of the church's history there was no dogmatic definition of the number of sacraments nor was there a clear consensus as to just what acts were considered sacraments. The number seven became accepted during the twelfth century because of a best-selling theology textbook, and it was dogmatically defined in the fifteenth century and reaffirmed in the sixteenth. But for well over a thousand years, i.e., most of our history, there was no agreement as to a precise list of sacraments. During this time dozens of different acts were called sacraments by various distinguished theologians. Augustine, for example, counted the baptismal font, the Creed, the Lord's Prayer, salt used in baptisms, and ashes in penance as sacraments. Obviously, a precise definition of the number of sacraments was not essential to the church's operation.

The Reformation brought a sharp confrontation on defining the sacraments. The conflict was not over the main consideration—that the sacraments consisted of "an outward and visible sign of an inward and spiritual grace"; both sides agreed on that. The conflict was over the qualification "ordained by Christ himself," i.e., having a divine promise found in scripture. Following the precedent of Luther, all the reformers argued that only baptism and the eucharist could be found specifically instituted by Christ in scripture. The Roman Catholic fathers at Trent insisted that no "more or fewer than seven" were "instituted by Jesus Christ our Lord" but shrewdly abstained from defining exactly where.

Both sides in the sixteenth-century controversy were operating with a biblical literalism that I find difficult to accept. Luther, for example, believed that we have the exact words of Christ in the accounts of the Last Supper or in Mark 16:16 and Matt. 28:19. Thus one could interpret "do this" as a command and "baptize men" as another dominical injunction. From what we know today of biblical studies, it is questionable whether we have preserved in either instance the exact words of Christ. Thus literalistic reliance on divine injunctions found verbatim in scripture as the basis for defining the number of sacraments seems dubious.

It is interesting to see Roman Catholic theologians raising similar questions. Karl Rahner points out "for four sacraments [matrimony, ordination, healing of the sick, and confirmation] we have no words of institution from Jesus Christ himself." [18] He goes on to point out that confirmation was once part of baptism and that ordination is threefold: to the diaconate,

---

[18] Karl Rahner, *The Church and the Sacraments* (London: Burns & Oates, 1964), p. 42.

priesthood, and episcopate. He claims that "what is essential about the definition that there are seven sacraments, is not the number, but the affirmation that the ecclesiastical rites comprised by this number are in fact of sacramental efficacy, all these and only these."[19] But one could say there are six sacraments or nine without saying "anything false." So there are some indications that the precise numbering of sacraments is now being treated a bit more openly among Roman Catholics.

I suggest that the number of sacraments should once again be considered an open question as it was for most of our history. The continued use, in various forms, of all seven rites by many Protestants testifies to their value in the life of the community of faith. I shall treat this question as open and not closed either by the biblical literalism of the reformers or the dogmatism of Trent. It is conceivable to me that the church will discover in its life together new ways in which God gives himself to us as love. The canon of sacraments, in theory at least, still ought to be open.

It is time for us to look at the sacraments individually. I shall follow the distinction mentioned above between sacraments in which relationships of love are established and those by which such relationships are maintained. I shall try to show how the church experiences both ways in which God gives himself to us. My treatment of individual sacraments will be brief but, I hope, will illustrate more specifically what I have just outlined about the sacraments in general.

II

Several of the sacraments function to establish new relationships of love within the community of faith. In these, God acts to bring about a change in our being by placing us in a new role with regard to others in the community. In several

---

[19]*Ibid.*, p. 56.

sacraments this has traditionally been called indelibility, resulting from the imparting of a new character. For this reason, baptism, confirmation, and ordination have been regarded as unrepeatable. A more dynamic view is that the new relationships, established by these sacraments, are intended to be lifelong and hence repetition of them (as contrasted to renewal) would be meaningless. The sacraments that establish these new relationships of love also involve a passage into a new role by separation from former allegiances (renunciation, "forsaking all others," etc.).

The first of the sacraments that establish new relationships is, naturally, that of Christian initiation. Christian initiation has always involved a variety of rites, but they have been related to one another in different ways among different churches. Generally baptism has been followed by laying-on-of-hands or sealing with oil and the process completed in first communion. Thus we could be dealing with three sacraments here. Instead, I shall deal with them as one sacrament, Christian initiation. I shall treat the eucharist in more detail later.

The establishment of a new relationship of love is apparent in initiation. In this sacrament, God places us where salvation becomes a possibility, inside his community of faith. The outsider becomes an insider: "You are now the people of God, who once were not his people" (I Pet. 2:10). Now we know the church from the inside. Our being has changed, for we approach the church no longer as strangers and aliens but incorporated into it as members of a chosen people. Our nurture and care become the loving concern of other members of the body. And we, in turn, are bound to build them up in conduct and faith.

God's action in this sacrament unites us to Jesus Christ through the sign-act of sharing in his death and resurrection in baptism (Rom. 6:3-5). Thus we can speak of God giving himself to us "when we were baptized into union with Christ Jesus" so that, united to Christ, all he accomplished is ours to offer. We renounce the world and its temptations, passing through this death of our past to new life in the community of faith.

The New Testament describes God's gifts to us in Christian initiation with a wonderful variety of images. Our sin is washed away in the sign-act of water baptism, and we emerge from the font or baptistery having been cleansed: "But you have been through the purifying waters; [you have been made holy] and justified through the name of the Lord Jesus and the Spirit of our God" (I Cor. 6:11; bracketed translation mine). This is obviously not for us to boast; it is God's forgiving gift. God's action is shown in the metaphor of our being born anew (John 3:5, Titus 3:5). This is also closely connected in the passages with the gift of the Holy Spirit. The New Testament speaks of God giving himself to us directly in initiation: "Repent and be baptized . . . and you will receive the gift of the Holy Spirit" (Acts 2:38). Elsewhere this divine self-giving is related to the sign-act of laying-on-of-hands (Acts 8:17-19; 19:6). For those newly baptized and who have just received the laying-on-of-hands, the welcome to the Lord's table represents the final act of welcome into the household of faith.

In matrimony the love of a man and a woman for each other is given visible and verbal form. The visual enactment often gets overlooked because of our fascination with words. But the clasping of hands and the giving to each other of worldly goods through the symbolism of the rings are more eloquent than words. In the wedding service a couple gives themselves to each other, making their relationship of love visible in the midst of a supportive community.

Here, too, God gives himself to us in providing an image of ideal love through Christ's self-giving love for the church, through his community that witnesses the vows and gives them a public reality, and through his own power in perfecting our love. God works through the couple, who themselves enact this sacrament. Matrimony is both intensely public in establishing a new relationship of responsible love within the supporting community and intensely private. One cannot be entirely satisfied with the decision of the medieval church that legitimate consent, the necessary substance for the sacrament, is expressed by spoken public vows alone rather than by the private marriage act itself. But the private consummation would have far less meaning without the community in which the public vows establish a new relationship of love.

I cannot help pondering what would have been the consequences if the Reformation had continued to think of marriage as a sacrament. Would the Christian assembly be more apt to nourish a couple's love if it really understood matrimony as a sacrament through which God gives himself to the community in establishing within it this new relationship of love? Would we be more inclined to build up the love of a couple in conflict rather than allowing them to walk away from each other? If we considered marriage as part of God's action through his church, would we be more concerned about this health of a part of the body of Christ than are the marriage clinics? It is worth considering.

Ordination establishes a new relationship of leadership within the community. Several things are at stake here. God gives himself to the community through calling individuals to minister and through providing them with the requisite gifts and graces. Thus ordination recognizes God's activity in providing leadership. Individuals are examined and proclaimed "worthy" of the responsibilities of leadership because of what God has already done in them by their call and gifts.

The community accepts the gift of leadership thankfully in confidence that each member of the body exercises his or her special gifts for the benefit of the whole. It is a relationship of love that God initiates through calling an individual to ministerial leadership. The church responds by giving thanks for this gift of God.

The church ratifies God's call and gifts by conferring its

authority on the individual. The Holy Spirit is invoked on those being ordained that they may share in the authority of the church by being given the authority of preaching and administering the sacraments as representatives of the church's faith. The calling and gifts that God has given and the church has certified thus make it possible for the community to designate a person as its representative. He or she is now authorized to preach the church's faith, administer its sacraments, and perform the office and work of a deacon, presbyter, or bishop for the building up of the community of faith.

There are some curious gaps in our sacramental life. I venture on controversial matters by suggesting that deficiencies here could be remedied by new sacraments establishing relationships besides the traditional ones. We have failed, for example, to express God's giving of himself to us in providing the calling and talents requisite for entering upon a secular vocation in the service of humanity. We have been inconsistent, not neglecting the fringes of vocation, but missing the center of the matter. We do commemorate God's self-giving act in calling people to a vocation of ministry. We celebrate the profession of monastic vows in a rite that was once considered a sacrament. And what has been known in the West as "confirmation" in some traditions recognizes the maturing of persons or the commissioning of baptized persons to serve humanity. But usually it comes at an age much too young to signify that such commissioning is fulfilled through a vocation.

How do we recognize the end of dependence and being served and the start of service to others through a vocation? We do not at present unless a person has a vocation to clerical or monastic life. Surely this contradicts the whole Protestant concept of a secular vocation as a calling to serve humanity. We commission clergy and monks but have equal reason to commission all others to a vocation of service. We fail to signify the acceptance of a vocation as the establishment of a relationship of love through which a member of the community of faith serves the whole human community.

Perhaps we would do well to think through the possibilities of a new sacrament of vocation. It might take suggestions from the vows of initiation, marriage, ordination, and monastic profession. Symbols of particular trades or professions could be given. Such a sacrament could recognize separation from the stage of life of being served and trained and progression to the service of others. It should recognize God's gift in calling us and giving us talents and skills to serve him through the vocation.

The burial of a Christian has not been considered a sacrament at any time that I know of, though it has often been commemorated through a eucharistic celebration. I think, though, that there are reasons to think of it in terms of a sacrament in its own right. It would be a sacrament of establishment, for through death the Christian moves to a new relationship within the community. Separation is obvious, but the beginning of a new relationship of love within the communion of the saints needs to be underscored. One does not leave the body of Christ by death but passes into a new relationship to its members, just as at other stages of life. Of course, a Christian's death and resurrection with Christ has been foreshadowed in baptism. It is unfortunate that we forget about baptism at burial, though the imagery and ideas of both are closely related as initiations into the church militant and triumphant.

God gives himself to us in the burial of a Christian in the gift of trust. In the face of death we are forced to accept the stark insufficiency of anything less than the trustworthiness of God. Christian burial is both a consolation to the mourners and a commendation to God of a member of the body of Christ. God gives himself to us in enabling us to trust that even death cannot "separate us from the love of God in Christ Jesus our Lord" (Rom. 8:39). Christian burial makes visible God's self-giving in incorporating even our death into his life and purpose.

The church responds to such gifts by giving God thanks for the life he has given. On this occasion, the Lord's Supper can become a fitting offering of thanksgiving. It is also an eloquent testimony to the unbroken fellowship of those united in the one body which death cannot diminish. Thus even death for a Christian is received with thanksgiving, and his or her burial becomes a moment of confident hope in a God who never ceases giving himself to us even at the graveside.

New relationships are established in initiation, matrimony, ordination, vocation, and Christian burial. There are also sacraments in which old relationships of love are maintained within the community of faith. These sacraments are repeatable. Their purpose is not the creation of new relationships but the maintenance of those already established. They sustain us rather than mark transitions.

I mention briefly baptismal renewal though not as a sacrament. There has been much recent interest in the renewal of baptism, though from early times this has been part of the Roman Catholic Easter vigil. Whether called baptismal renewal, affirmation of baptismal vows, or affirmation of the baptismal covenant this is regarded not as a sacrament but as a way of maintaining awareness of the relationship our baptism originally established. This relationship is sustained by renewal of it, by repristination.

Baptismal renewal is not rebaptism. Rebaptism is a form of blasphemy, for it states that God did not keep his promises to us in baptism, that God failed, that he gave himself in vain. Baptismal renewal, on the other hand, with its stress on "remember your baptism and be thankful," is a fresh reminder to us of what God has already done for us.

The Lord's Supper is a sacrament that maintains relationships of love. As we have seen, when joined to baptism and laying-on-of-hands it can also be part of establishing a new relationship. In the Lord's Supper, God gives himself to us in the most direct and personal way. Just as Jesus Christ gave his body and blood for us in "historical visibility," so here he continues to give himself for us in the breaking of bread and drinking of wine. The use of bread and wine "God into man conveys" and "fills his faithful people's hearts with all the life of God." It is a mystery that surpasses our ability to comprehend and our power to express, but not our capacity to experience. In the giving of bread and wine, God gives himself to us just as any gift conveys the giver. The feeble elements undergo a real change, for they bear a new meaning, that of God giving himself to us. They are no longer mere bread and wine, for they have acquired a new significance and embody Christ's giving of himself.

We can speak of this giving in several ways. We experience God's gift of himself in making us one with Christ and one with one another as we share in one loaf of bread and cup of wine. We experience his giving himself in the reading and preaching of his word. (Thus it is not necessary to consider preaching a separate sacrament since it is part of the Lord's Supper.) He makes his gift known through the ministry of others. And he gives himself through our actions of giving thanks over bread and wine as we make memorial of Christ's sacrifice for us.

Throughout life we renew our relationship of love by participating in this visible sign-act of God's love. As bread and wine are used, they become the extraordinary within the ordinary, the vehicle through which God the Son gives himself to us. We experience for ourselves the same saving will visible in Bethlehem, Nazareth, and Jerusalem. The objects and actions are completely imbued with Christ's own activity. Our love is built up as the Lord gives himself to us so that we can give ourselves for others. Love is made visible in us as well.

Great changes have been made in recent years both in the concept and practice of the sacrament of anointing of the sick. From the last-ditch stand that extreme unction implied, it has become, instead, the sacrament of healing. In its early and biblical sense it was indeed a sacrament of the love of the community made visible: "Is one of you ill? He should send for the elders of the congregation to pray over him and anoint him with oil in the name of the Lord. . . . Confess your sins to one another, and pray for one another, and then you will be healed" (James 5:14-16). Healing, then, is a concern of the whole community of faith in which its love for a member is made visible.

Mutual confession is linked with healing, for relationships of love demand an honesty and a peace of conscience. Unfortunately, the medieval church placed almost all its concern on "the healing of the mind" to the neglect of much sense of participation of the community through maintaining the relationship of love through intercessory prayer. The act of anointing may signify less in English than in languages where *anoint, Christ, chrism, Messiah* are obviously related terms. But the sign value of the community ministering through prayer is no less diminished.

God gives himself to us in the possibility of healing and through the visible sign of concern and ministry of the community. Love in action becomes visible as the church unites to seek the restoration to health of any member of its body. Since this sacrament can be repeated and intercession may be prolonged, I prefer to think of it as a way of maintaining a relationship of love.

The sacrament of reconciliation (frequently called confession or penance) also represents an act of healing. This was more conspicuous in the early church where the notorious sin of a Christian could imperil the survival of a congregation in pagan culture. Anyone guilty of flagrant sin offended God and created a wound in the body that hurt the whole local Christian community. Reconciliation was a long process of healing in which the offender was restored to health through the ministry of the total community. It was by no means a private sacrament, though it became such increasingly in the early middle ages.

Reconciliation, then, is an act through which God heals us by reuniting us to one another. We have a suggestion of this in the giving of the peace in the eucharist. In the sacrament of reconciliation we are led to examine ourselves and the ways in which we break the bonds of love. This may demand specifically recalling types and number of transgressions. A general confession all too easily becomes an evasion by not being personal and specific. Yet our offenses are individual and concrete as well as social. This is the bitter medicine of reconciliation.

But God acts to give us his forgiving love, and we are healed by him through the ministry of the community which reunites us to one another. It is a continuing process of sickness and restoration to health, sin, and forgiveness. Reconciliation is a sacrament of maintenance enacted through the community as a visible sign of love. The Vietnam war made many Protestant congregations see the importance of the sacrament of reconciliation as we realized our social sin. But this experience did not always make clear that God gives himself as "heavenly medicine" to heal us in reconciliation and that this is indeed good news, the news of a forgiven prodigal, an invalid restored to health. The wounds that hurt one another are healed through the forgiveness God gives in reuniting us.

I have described eight sign-acts through which the Christian community can see God's love visible within its life. In each of these, but in differing ways, God acts to establish or to maintain relationships of love within the church.

I do not mean to suggest that these are the only ways. There are no limits to the uncovenanted mercies of God or to our ignorance of them. I have only tried to describe briefly eight ways in which the church can experience the sacraments as God acting in self-giving love to create or to renew our relationships of love within his community.

III

Starting from Our Tradition

None of us comes to the planning of worship without a history, though we may or may not be aware of that history. Our history can either enslave us or liberate us. It will enslave us if we do not know our past, for unknown history will dictate our choices and limit our possibilities without our knowledge. But the history we know can liberate us by showing us how our perspectives have been shaped by the past and how we can transcend such limitation. If we recognize the type of glasses through which we see worship, we can be conscious of how they color what we see.

We soon discover how our own identity is based on the paths Western Catholicism trod and on the paths not taken. We recognize that Western Catholicism represents only one of several ancient and present-day possibilities, and that at least six other centers of liturgical development have existed or still remain in such ancient Christian centers as Egypt, western Syria, eastern Syria, Asia Minor, Constantinople, and scattered over northern Italy, France, Spain, and Ireland. However partial they are, the possibilities most of us are familiar with were determined by the history of that segment of Christianity centered in Rome.

We must also recognize how we have been determined by the approaches to worship developed by the reformers and their successors. However confined our own segment of history is, it is the one we must appropriate first before we venture further.

Everyone who plans to make a big leap forward needs to have a secure footing before he or she jumps. Everyone who plans worship brings along a history, but only those who know that history are free to go beyond it. Any important step forward must begin with a backward look so as to gain self-knowledge. We start out from within our own tradition after we have become aware of the ways in which our tradition has both strengthened and limited us. It is my purpose in this chapter to present an overview of Protestant worship with the hope of providing a useful instrument for self-understanding.

I believe that virtually all Protestant worship falls within one of seven traditions. Some might prefer to call these "families," as is often done with classical liturgical families. The problem with this term is that usage has so long linked "families" with written documents that it is hard to give it a broader meaning. By "traditions" I mean inherited bodies of habits and assumptions as well as documents and practices. Some of these traditions can easily be defined in terms of service books; for others, that norm is totally inapplicable. And whereas classical liturgical families have usually been discerned in terms of the eucharist, this is not feasible for some Protestant traditions.

We must therefore find a better basis for defining a worship tradition than the relationships within a family of eucharistic rites. I propose to do this by trying to define the ethos of each Protestant worship tradition. Obviously some will be much harder to characterize than others. But I think in each case certain dominant characteristics can be recognized as distinctive earmarks of such a tradition. The ethos of each tradition is determined by such varied factors as the use of service books or their lack; stress on the sacraments or the absence of such emphasis; tendency to uniformity or to pluralism; autonomy or interconnection; the importance and function of music and the other arts; ceremonial or its absence; unifying sources within the tradition; and theological, historical, and sociological factors. I shall attempt primarily, in the short space available here, to describe the dominant characteristics of each tradition rather than try to depict its history. Obviously the two cannot be completely separated. Characterization will inevitably be more subjective than a straight historical account. But my present purpose is to be descriptive, not historical.

To simplify matters, the dominant relationships between traditions may be visualized through the chart below. More radical developments are on the left. The first four traditions originated in the sixteenth century; tradition 5, in the seventeenth century; 6, in the eighteenth; and 7, in the twentieth. The downward direction of the lines indicates the chief directions of liturgical influence.

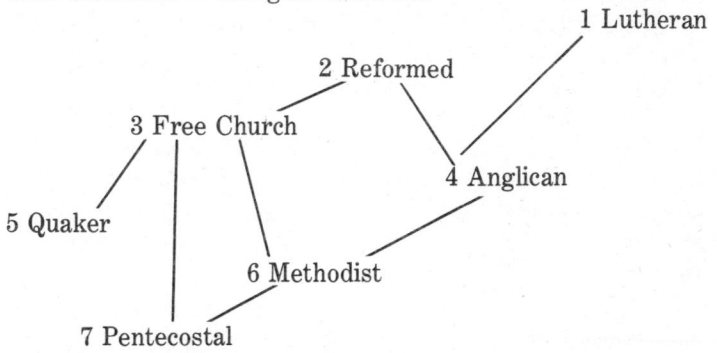

Each line indicates only the strongest original impetus. In time, many of the relationships became reciprocal: Methodist hymnody influenced Anglican worship, Scottish Presbyterians adopted Free Church pew communion, Methodist preaching affected Free Church preaching. But the chart should be of some help in making comparisons as to origins.

I

The first of our liturgical traditions is the Lutheran. Its dominant characteristic seems to be a strong conservatism with a few rather radical elements thrown in for a delightful inconsistency. In a word, it is largely a lengthened shadow of

Martin Luther himself as pastor, scholar, and reformer. When pastors today resist changes for fear they may upset the faithful, they could easily quote Luther's concern that the laity might be troubled by the innovations of Carlstadt. Yet, at the same time, Luther instigated some drastic changes. His treatise *The Babylonian Captivity of the Church* (1520) set the pattern for virtually all Protestant worship: only two sacraments, communion in both kinds, transubstantiation repudiated, and the mass not a sacrifice. But it must be remembered that Luther's first attempt at a mass, the *Formula Missae* of 1523, was in Latin and drastic only when it got to the canon. The *Deutsche Messe* of 1526 went further, though many segments of Lutheranism patterned their eucharistic rite after the earlier and more conservative version. In this case, we can speak of a Lutheran liturgical family, or rather of two closely related families. The most distinctive family likeness is the absence of a canon. Even this distinction disappeared among many American Lutherans in 1958.

A second feature, not anticipated by Luther, was the slow deterioration of the sacramental life and of the ceremonial that accompanied it. In Sweden these elements lasted until the onset of the Enlightenment in the eighteenth century. The fore-mass came to be the dominant Sunday service in Lutheran parishes and has stood the test of time with little change. The offices, by comparison, withered into insignificance. A strong emphasis on preaching has always characterized Lutheran worship, but this form of Christ's presence has not detracted from the sense of his real presence in the eucharist even when the eucharist became infrequent.

A third and vital characteristic of Lutheran worship has been its warm hospitality to the arts, especially music. Luther fostered this attitude by writing about thirty-seven hymns himself and by encouraging composers to write for the church. Almost all traditions of worship have been enriched by

Lutheran composers, of whom Bach was only the most eminent. Lutheran countries were spared much of the iconoclasm that devastated churches in other lands. Today, Lutheran churches in the Midwest reflect the best in contemporary church architecture more consistently than those of any other tradition.

Worship in the Reformed tradition has shown less consistency and is more difficult to characterize. Certainly it was less conservative originally than Lutheran worship and, perhaps as a result, has been more free to change during its history. Part of the diffuseness of the Reformed tradition comes from the fact that it originated chiefly in three centers under three quite different leaders: Zwingli in Zurich, Bucer in Strasbourg, and Calvin in Geneva. Of these three men, I would consider Martin Bucer the key leader in shaping Reformed worship.

If there is any obvious feature of Reformed worship, it is the strong emphasis on the supremacy of the word of God. This is evident not only in the dominance of the sermon but also in the way that hymnody and prayer tend to become means of proclaiming God's word. Singing was long restricted to psalmody and still is in some places, and the "long prayer" tended to be a short sermon. Much of Reformed worship in sixteenth-century liturgies appears to us as boringly didactic, and it still seems characteristic of worship in this tradition to be the most determinedly intellectual of those we meet. Discipline under God's word, too, long dominated Reformed worship, as is evident from the prominence of the Decalogue and the fencing of tables at communion. A deep sense of humanity's sinfulness and personal introspection seem to prevail.

It is more difficult to define a liturgical family in this instance, though the funnel through which Reformed worship poured into many lands was John Calvin's *Form of Church Prayers* of 1542. This work relies heavily on the Strasbourg reformers, especially Bucer. Almost immediately there began a rapid disintegration of the sacramental life (contrary to Calvin's wishes) and the disappearance of much ceremonial (in accordance with his desires). The basic Sunday service became the fore-mass, although less and less recognizable as it was adapted for different countries. Some family likenesses persist with regularity: the use of the Decalogue for self-examination, a prayer for illumination before the scriptures are read, minimal ceremonial, and a general tendency to wordiness. When the eucharist is celebrated, the words of institution from I Corinthians 11 are read as a "warrant" outside the eucharistic prayer. This in itself is symptomatic: The eucharist, though older than the written scriptures, still needs to be authorized by the pronunciation of God's word of command for it.

It is not surprising that the arts were neglected. The invention of the printing press and the stress on verbal perception had made the other visual arts less exciting and necessary. Literacy and Reformed worship went hand in hand. Yet there is a fine austerity in much Reformed worship that is far more attractive than the gush of nineteenth-century sentimentality which often overwhelmed such restraint.

This tradition has accepted change more readily than some. After about eighty years the Scots abandoned fixed liturgies in 1645 until, in the nineteenth century, Dr. Lee was censured for reading prayers from a book. Hymnody was eventually accepted in many areas. Recent years have seen a recovery of some of the Reformed liturgies of the past and an effort to restore a strong sacramental life.

Our third tradition is so diffuse that some might argue that it has no consistency at all. Even the name I have chosen, Free Church, is open to debate. Some might say it is a tradition of no tradition. Yet I would argue that there are some common characteristics that can be found in groups from widely varied theological, geographical, and historical backgrounds.

I would say that the first quality of the Free Church tradition is the autonomy of the local congregation in ordering its own worship. This not only means the freedom to use fixed formularies but also, more often than not, an inclination against so doing. Some traditions can almost be defined by the way they use a service book—for some (Lutheran, Anglican) it is mandatory, for others (Reformed, Methodist) it is recommended but voluntary. In the Free Church tradition, only the local church can make this determiniation.

Behind this autonomy is a deeper concern, the desire to be free to follow God's word. This has often led to a deep suspicion of all that is not provided for in scripture, including the refusal to use fixed prayer, hymns, and ceremonies. The problem is, of course, that people could not agree on what was provided for in God's word with regard to worship, and there was a temptation to make the Bible just as legalistic as any service book. We can cite three quite distinct varieties of Free Church worship, yet with common features.

The sixteenth-century Anabaptists represented an underground church in resistance to the state churches. Their worship was one of extreme simplicity though of much variety. Some developed a great hymnody; others thought this an affectation, for one should speak directly to God. For some the Lord's Supper was not spiritual enough; yet most groups practiced it. They did agree, however, that on the basis of scripture, believers alone should be baptized.

The English Puritans, or at least most of them, agreed that the baptism of infants was agreeable to God's word. They set out to complete the Reformation by going further than Calvin, who had halted short of eliminating all unscriptural ceremonies, or Cranmer, who had retained too many relics "culled and picked out of that popish dunghill, the mass book full of all abominations." Their worship was to be made "agreeable to God's word," not to human invention. Some even deplored the "vain repetitions" of the Lord's Prayer, though it certainly was scriptural enough. When they put it all together, it became the *Westminster Directory* adopted by Parliament in 1645. The *Directory* was a service book consisting entirely of rubrics.

A third variety of the Free Church tradition is the Disciples of Christ, who resolved, this time in nineteenth-century America, to avoid all that the scriptures avoid. This standard got rid of such things as creeds. But it did produce a recognition of the centrality of the Lord's Supper in the New Testament, and the Disciples became the first Protestant group both to recover and to retain weekly communion. They, too, found no scriptural warrant for the baptism of infants.

Perhaps it is not surprising that the Free Church tradition is the most widespread in America, though divided in many ways. This tradition is represented among groups as varied as Mennonites, Baptists, Churches of Christ, United Church of Christ, Christian Church (Disciples of Christ), and many others. And it has had strong influence on the other traditions except the Lutheran and Anglican.

The most coherent and easily defined tradition of all is the Anglican tradition. Essentially it is the tradition of the *Book of Common Prayer*, though this gives a far broader scope than one might at first suspect. Basically most of the dominant features of Anglican worship appear in the 1549 Prayer Book and in the sudden lurch to the left of the 1552 book. Except for the Scottish book, subsequent national books have been channeled through the English Prayer Book of 1662. The inherent strength of Cranmer's 1549 Prayer Book is shown in the long survival of many of its services with a minimum of change. Even the latest American version (with the exception of baptism and confirmation) preserves a strong continuity with 1549. And even more remarkable has been the degree to which, despite fervent theological and ecclesiastical battles, the Prayer Book has continued to be the source of unity for Anglicans. In recent years it has been a bit amazing to see many Roman Catholic priests experiment rather freely with various unauthorized liturgies while their Anglican brothers and sisters adhere faithfully to the Prayer Book services and authorized alternatives.

No doubt much of the strength of the Prayer Book is in the catholicity of its sources and the moderate temper of Thomas Cranmer in selecting so widely and so discreetly. Not only did this Archbishop of Canterbury blend the service books of Sarum with the proposals of people as varied as Cardinal Quiñones, Luther, and Bucer, but he also managed to compress a variety of service books into a single volume usable by laity and clergy alike. Thus the judicious balance of the Prayer Book and the relative freedom it allows with regard to theological interpretation are undoubtedly basic properties of Anglican worship.

The Prayer Book also left a wide range to the discretion of the parish priest with regard to architectural setting, ceremonial, vestments, and the like. It is easily forgotten that the romanticism of the nineteenth century brought back much of the architecture, ceremonial, and vestments of the middle ages that had been absent from Anglicanism for over two centuries. Indeed, chancels, chants, and chasubles had as little appeal to Anglicans in the eighteenth century as they did to members of the Reformed tradition. But the important fact is that the Prayer Book was compatible with these things when they became desirable in the 1840s and undesirable in the 1970s.

Some of the most distinctive aspects of the Anglican ethos were neither planned nor desired by the reformers. Cranmer succeeded too well with morning and evening prayer, and their rich combination of scripture with congregational participation became the basic staple of Anglican worship for three hundred years instead of the eucharist. In a sense, the Lutheran and Reformed traditions, by clinging to the fore-mass as the normal service, were a bit more conservative than the Anglican, which unintentionally made the divine office primary. Cranmer's omission of hymnody was partly due to a justified modesty on his part when it came to versifying and the absence of others to write hymns. Not till the mid–nineteenth century was hymnody introduced into Anglicanism. Even then it was attacked as being "Methodistical," though early Anglican hymnals contained many hymns medieval in origin.

Cranmer's literary skills in prose were so enormous that generations have thrilled to the beauty of the Prayer Book even when "sore let and hindered" from comprehending it all. There has developed a tradition within Anglicanism of reveling in "our incomparable liturgy" that has been a conserving factor and has led the Church of England to use the 1662 revision for over three hundred years. This, in turn, made for a certain Anglican assurance about worship, often the envy of other traditions, but a liability today in a world of liturgical change.

The Quaker tradition may be as easy to distinguish as the Anglican, but is unlike it in every other way. Not only is there no service book, there may be no words at all. For Quakers, or Society of Friends, the dominant characteristic of worship is the silent waiting on God.

In one sense, Quaker worship was a culmination of the Free Church desire to complete the Reformation of worship. The Puritans, the Quakers felt, had lopped off the branches and not laid the axe to the root. Sermons and pastoral prayers were still human inventions, designed to impress human hearers rather than God. And scripture itself was secondhand when the Source of inspiration was directly open to all people who would listen. So the Quakers not only dispensed with the rubrics which the Puritans had retained but went beyond scripture. It is no wonder that in the 1640s George Fox was persecuted by his Puritan contemporaries.

Yet Quaker worship is deceptive, for it is highly disciplined and reflects a lifetime of practice. I know of no other tradition which so cherishes birthright memberships. It takes discipline to learn not to rush into words, to center down, to wait upon God, and to speak from the group. Quaker worship is a corporate form of mysticism. Robert Barclay, the theologian of the second generation of Quakers (a man fond of quoting Bernard of Clairvaux), spoke of Quaker worship as producing more light, just as many candles do when burning together. The inner light is given to share, and so it is necessary to meet. And the inner light is given to all alike, though soon wounded to death by most people. The Quakers were the first to insist that women's concerns be heard in meetings, and the Quakers first opposed slavery. The absence of clergy has been another sign of equality among most Quakers.

With their insistence on the Spirit speaking to the group through individual members, there seems to be no need for such visibles as bread and wine and water. So the Quakers commune on Christ inwardly and receive the baptism of the Holy Spirit without outward and visible forms. They stand as a forceful challenge to much recent thinking about the value of sign-acts; yet they have certainly never been deficient in the sign value of their acts of charity outside the meetinghouse. It is quite possible that the Quakers have remained the least changed of all Protestant worship traditions, though the most radical of all in their seventeenth-century origins. A few congregations in the Midwest have employed clergy and moved into the Free Church stream, but most Quaker worship has remained faithful to its origins.

The Methodist tradition developed in a different century and in a situation difficult to characterize. In some ways, early Methodism resembled a religious order within Anglicanism and even included obedience to a rule. Early Methodist worship in England combined a formal eucharistic life with the informality of field preaching, joyful hymnody, and extempore prayer. In many ways it was a blend of Anglican and Free

Church traditions seasoned with a strong dose of pragmatism. John Wesley, Methodism's founder, had catholic tastes like Cranmer. He drew on his patristic scholarship, Moravian pietism, the Church of England, and the Puritans to make a marvelous synthesis of evangelical and sacramental forms of worship. Unfortunately, Wesley's strong eucharistic piety did not survive his generation or weather the trip across the Atlantic. Soon forgotten was the collection of eucharistic hymns by John and Charles Wesley which emphasized the real presence and the eucharist as sacrifice.

The other side of Methodism developed—the folksy side with its fervent preaching, warm hymn-singing, and ardent, extempore prayer. Bishop Francis Asbury refounded Methodism in America without Wesley's refinements or Wesley's love of the *Book of Common Prayer*. Asbury and many of his clergy preferred to pray with their eyes and books shut. The Free Church tradition was to exert an increasing influence on Methodism as Wesley's 1784 revision of the Prayer Book was forgotten except for the "Sacramental Services, &c.": baptism of infants and those of riper years, holy communion, weddings, funerals, the ordinal and, eventually, services for laying a cornerstone and dedicating a church and for receiving people into church membership. For these occasional services Methodists again became people of the book. But the rest of the time local autonomy prevailed as with most churches on the frontier. Yet Methodism's involvement in evangelistic preaching was to reshape considerably the worship of many segments of the Free Church tradition. Only the hymnody and style of preaching distinguished Methodist worship from its Free Church neighbors, and even these distinctions rapidly melted in nineteenth-century America.

Hymnody plays such an important role in Methodist worship that it stands as a distinctive trait. It must be remembered that English-speaking Protestantism sang only psalms in the eighteenth century and that Isaac Watts was regarded as a dangerous innovator for trying to improve on King David. The English language was ripe for metrical hymns, and Charles Wesley's sixty-five hundred hymns are Methodism's greatest gift to Christian worship.

Our last tradition, the Pentecostal, was born with the twentieth century. I would say that its dominant characteristic is the freedom and spontaneity with which any worshiper can testify, sing, pray, speak in tongues, or interpret. There is the same sense of the Spirit-filled congregation that we find in Quaker worship, though I am not aware of any historical linkage of the two. The differences from Quaker worship—for example, visible sacraments, singing, preaching—are numerous. Nor do I include Pentecostal worship within the Free Church tradition, since the latter usually assumes a specific order of worship, even if local in origin, and the minister usually controls the entire service. If there are historical antecedents, they probably are found in the revival services and prayer meetings that prevailed in both Methodist and Free Church worship in nineteenth-century America.

In recent years Pentecostalism has shown up where least expected, among Catholic college students. Historically it has been centered among the economically and culturally deprived. It is the one tradition in which blacks have shared leadership from the first. Black worship, particularly in the Free Church and Methodist traditions, has tended to derive from that of the white majority. The chief black contributions appear to be in hymnody and in preaching. At present, Pentecostalism is the most rapidly growing of all seven traditions, especially in Africa and South America.

It may seem fatuous to speak of a "tradition" only three quarters of a century old. But within the enormous diversity of Pentecostal worship certain constants appear, and the term "classical Pentecostalism" is already in vogue to distinguish the older variety from "neo-Pentecostalism." Glossolalia is the most striking phenomenon of the Pentecostal tradition. But even more important is the unexpected possibility of spontaneous worship. For these people, worship does not mean the sequential movement through an order, as most Catholic and Protestant worship implies, but rather it means following the movement of the Spirit. Clergy provide leadership, but always subject to what seems like interruption to outsiders but in reality is the heart of the service. Informality has finally triumphed in Pentecostal worship.

Pentecostalism has within recent years shown the possibility of breaking out of its sociological limitations in this country and of assuming an important political role in crusading for social justice in other countries. Its most creative years may still lie ahead. When combined with a deep sacramentalism, it can produce a very catholic tradition of worship. There are signs that this is happening in various places among both Protestants and Catholics. It is to the credit of the Roman Catholic bishops of this country that they have been open to these possibilities.

II

Today we see a new phenomenon, the coalescence of once disparate traditions and intermarriage between many families of worship. Thus what were once distinctive features of individual traditions now seem shared by all. And Catholicism is part of the picture too. Borrowing from the Eastern churches is practiced increasingly, though not reciprocated.

An early expression of the new ecumenical situation was seen in the Church of South India, where adherents of Anglican, Methodist, Free Church and Reformed traditions brought their own offerings together to form a new eucharistic rite in 1950 and its 1954 revision. They went further and adopted some indigenous Indian Christian elements from the Eastern churches. The result was far more than the sum of the individual parts; it made visible the new ecumenical era in worship. On the American scene a similar visibility has been reflected in the Consultation on Church Union (COCU) services.

It is quite possible that the greatest differences will soon be discernible within groups that previously would have been reckoned distinct traditions. Thus we would see several types of catholicity, slightly flavored by the historical experiences of each group.

At any rate, the liturgical pluralism of Protestantism now seems to be something for which we ought to give thanks and rejoice. Now that we are no longer defensive about our own tradition and suspicious of those of others, we can all share both the richness of the last four and a half centuries of liturgical experimentation and the wealth of the preceding centuries of Christian worship. And then we can all move ahead with one another's help.

IV

Reaching Our Culture

We start thinking about worship by becoming aware of our own tradition and how it has made us think as we do. But worship can also be heavily influenced by the culture in which we live. It is important for us to realize how this shapes our thinking too. We are using "culture" here in the sense that H. Richard Niebuhr did in defining it as "that total process of human activity and that total result of such activity."[1] More specifically, I shall discuss the effects of American culture on how we have been accustomed to think about worship. I shall be concerned not only with how we reach our culture but also with how we avoid getting lost in it. By reflecting on changes in both worship and culture in America we can see possibilities and problems.

Some groups, of course, have resisted contact with American culture in their worship. The Quaker tradition is too small and the Pentecostal too recent to tell much about how they have reflected American culture. The more conservative Anglican and Lutheran traditions have usually resisted too close contact with the mainstreams of American culture. There was a period in the nineteenth century when a portion of Anglicanism represented a counter-cultural movement. A large number of Anglicans in England and America professed to find more of value in a return to the middle ages than in the current cult of progress.[2]

It is the central traditions—Methodist, Reformed, and Free Church—that have reflected most consistently the changing cultural patterns of America during the last one hundred

---

[1] *Christ and Culture* (New York: Harper, 1951), p. 32.
[2] Cf. my *Cambridge Movement* (Cambridge: Cambridge University Press, 1962).

years. This segment, which I call "central Protestantism," will provide my chief examples of the relation of worship and cultural changes.

Before I begin, a word is necessary about the desirability of reaching our culture too successfully. How far do you go in reflecting a culture without simply being a mirror of it? How desirable is it to shed light on a culture by being a beacon shining from a distance? Those of us who live in the South have frequent opportunity to observe just how much Southern folk religion reflects in its worship all the limitations and glories of local culture. It is sometimes difficult to tell a naturalization ceremony in the courthouse from a service at a local church. The theologically conservative churches tend to mimic the culture of conservative regions and segments of America. Americanism and Christian worship sometimes become hard to distinguish, especially with flag processions and patriotic songs. Theologically liberal churches also seem equally sensitive to local culture and all too readily become mirrors of the segments of culture they represent.

There are both advantages and disadvantages to this situation. The whole relationship of worship to culture is highly ambiguous. We certainly do not desire the remoteness of Roman Catholic worship before Vatican II or of the Hutterites, whose sermons were all written in the sixteenth century. Worship can be relevant to all cultures, and it is important to reach people in their here and now. In short, worship needs to be relevant. On the other hand, there are dangers in perverting worship by too close assimilation to culture. A service which is a rally in support of American policy in Vietnam and one devoted exclusively to assailing such policy are both questionable as authentic worship. Cultural captivity is one of the hardest things to recognize, since we are so oblivious as to how it makes us think as we do. Authenticity to the Christian faith is also important in worship. Too great attention to relevancy alone may blind us to authenticity.

Perhaps we can best become aware of how our culture affects how we think by looking at the course of worship in central Protestantism during the last hundred years in America. To do this, we must avoid the smugness of the present; we must realize that we tend to do, as did our predecessors before us, what the times seem to call for, what our culture dictates. An awareness of this can help make us more critical of why we think as we think.

I

The past one hundred years show four rather different cultural eras in American history, reflected by four distinct eras in Protestant worship. For the first half of the past century, the period from 1875 to 1920, the dominant pattern of worship in central Protestantism showed the strong impact of revivalism. Worship tended to become a means to an end, the making of converts and the nourishing of those already converted. With such a purpose in mind, it became possible to shape worship to a practical and purposeful end, i.e., it worked. Whatever criticisms we may have of the effects of nineteenth-century revivalism upon worship, we cannot overlook its pragmatic character. A century earlier, Jonathan Edwards had written his *Faithful Narrative of the Surprising Work of God* (1737). Almost exactly a hundred years later appeared Charles G. Finney's *Lectures on Revivals of Religion* (1835). Edwards chronicles with amazement; Finney's book is a how-to manual, with the results almost guaranteed if one follows the proper techniques. Plant the proper grain, and the wheat will appear.

Finney's book could well stand as the prime example of this period in worship. Bold, brusk, and vigorous, he traces changes in worship, only to show that nothing has abided long and therefore the preacher is free to ignore history and to introduce "new measures" that will be effective. Behind all this is the pragmatic optimism of the time. America had been liberated from the dead hand of the past, and the future was dazzling. Call it manifest destiny, the age of reform, the frontier spirit, Horatio Alger, it had one thrust: use the right techniques and there was no limit to what could be accomplished.

Let us not be negative about the degree to which it worked. It made Christian a nation whose founding fathers had hardly been godly, righteous, or sober, despite myths to the contrary. And it gave vigor to dozens of reform movements including abolition. But it did have its faults, though today, after reacting against revivalism for half a century, we can see some of its virtues as well.

Its chief fault was that theologically it was weak. Dividing humanity into the saved and the lost does simplify things considerably. But there are contradictions in the phrase "bringing souls to Christ." And trying to snatch them from outer darkness into the bright radiance of salvation by an instantaneous occurrence caused problems. Some groups neglected children until they were ripe for conversion, and the passion for recruiting the outsider tended to overwhelm the care and discipline of those within the fold. The traditional means of grace were too easily replaced by more sensational new measures.

But theologically weak as it was, revivalism had some elements of keen psychological insight that we have had to relearn in the last ten years. For one thing, revivalism knew that in order to move people spiritually you have to move them physically. The church music which we told people for years was not good for them (and they still requested) was based on the realization that music is a body art. Even more important was the element of spontaneity, the unexpected possibility in worship. When the *Hymnal of the Methodist Episcopal*

Church in a printing of 1896 (or soon thereafter) first included an "Order of Public Worship," there was an outcry against such unfamiliar formality. Is it any wonder that older people in our churches have a curious nostalgia for the worship of this period, no matter how hard seminary-trained clergy discourage such hankering after the fleshpots of Egypt? Revivalism may have been theologically weak, but it understood people and did a fine job of reflecting many of the dominant currents of nineteenth-century American culture.

But cultural currents were changing, and the 1920s saw a new era emerging in worship too. I would call this the era of respectability and would divide it into two periods: one a period of aestheticism, the other a period of historicism. The era of respectability in Protestant worship was roughly the half century beginning in the early 1920s. It represents the assertion of sobriety over the ecstatic, of refinement over the primitive, of restraint over the boisterous. It was a reflection of the increased sophistication of Americans as education became available to most. There was a neat correlation between the changes in the educational level of the average central Protestant and what was happening to his worship life. The displays of emotion, the freedom, and spontaneity, the general folksiness of revivalism were all pushed aside or left behind for those who had not yet ascended the social and educational scale.

The first half of our period of respectability, roughly 1920 to 1945, saw a substitution for worship as a conversion experience (or renewal of such an experience) of worship as an aesthetic experience. The slogan, despite its inherent contradiction, was "enriching our worship." America is dotted with churches, usually Gothic where the budget would allow, that reflect both the wealth and the sophistication of the period. These are examples of the second Gothic revival—not the robust and original Gothic of the 1840s and 1850s but the academically correct Gothic of the 1920s. The buildings contain accurate copies of medieval elements, correct, timid, and in good taste. For good taste had invaded the sanctuary and replaced the pragmatic, functional, though hopelessly unsophisticated, Akron plan. Good taste had invaded the choir loft and replaced the folksy quartet or octet with a full-fledged choir singing "good" music by composers all a century safely dead. Good taste had created a formal order of worship, so that Methodists, for example, by 1932 had several orders of worship to choose from and by 1944 a whole *Book of Worship.* And with the mimeograph, no one had to worry about saying the right thing. No chances to take, no risks, just read your lines. One could be secure in confidence that nothing unexpected or chancy would happen in worship. It was all very respectable. My home-town church built a new stone Gothic building in the 1920s and immediately decided to forbid congregational "amens" during the sermon.

I believe that during the first half of this period worship came to be understood as akin to an aesthetic experience by many ministers and lay people. Probably the most representative book was Von Ogden Vogt's *Art & Religion,* published in 1921 and subsequently in 1929, 1948, and 1960.[3] Pastor of a Unitarian church in Chicago for two decades, Vogt was vigorously opposed to creedalism and dogmatism of any kind and could anticipate many of our contemporaries in defining "worship as the celebration of life" by advocating a "substitute Scripture reading taken from modern sources" and through using a variety of art forms. The experience of beauty and the experience of religion seemed remarkably similar to him. The arts served to help the worshiper "to be reverent and to display to him the larger cause of religion."[4] Vogt advised

---

[3] (New Haven: Yale University Press, 1921, 1929; Boston: Beacon Press, 1948, 1960.)

[4] Rev. ed. (1948), p. 53.

ministers to select "from the materials of the past those treasures which are least burdened with abandoned concepts."[5]

For many, public worship became an art form itself. Tremendous efforts were made in raising the "quality" of church music. A growing concern about church architecture was reflected in the creation of denominational building agencies. The use of classical prayers instead of spontaneous ones increased considerably. Books were written on "the art" of public worship.[6]

The warm glow of the conversion experience (or its memory) had been replaced for many by the more refined thrill of aesthetic experience. Here there was no risk of spontaneous emotion, no danger of exposing oneself by outward commitment. It was worship in good form, in which nothing overmuch prevailed. It was, in short, middle-class America with its primary values of security and comfort. Worship could continue to be a meaningful though highly subjective experience, without the risks of self-disclosure that revivalism demanded. If you could no longer tap your feet to the music, you could no longer do a lot of things in the big city that you did back in small-town America. So once again worship tended to mirror the values of the prevailing culture.

But the culture did not stand still, and neither did the forms of our worship. The years after World War II saw a quite different interest in worship in which the dominant phrase was "recovering our heritage," a phrase not without self-contradictions. I remember how much this era troubled Vogt,

---

[5] *Modern Worship* (New Haven: Yale University Press, 1927), p. 39.

[6] Albert Palmer, *The Art of Conducting Public Worship* (New York: Macmillan, 1939); Percy Dearmer, *The Art of Public Worship* (London: Mowbray, 1919); Scott Brenner, *The Art of Worship* (New York: Macmillan, 1961); Andrew Blackwood, *The Fine Art of Public Worship* (Nashville: Abingdon Press, 1939).

how much he regarded it as regression to a dark age of creedalism and dogmatism. It still remained a period of respectability both in worship and in American culture in general. But the thrust in worship was quite different, and aestheticism came to be looked at with real suspicion as hopelessly insufficient.

It must be remembered that the late forties and fifties were a period of great growth in the American churches, a tendency that lost momentum in the 1960s. Attempts were frequently made, and with some justice, to connect this growth in church membership with the age of anxiety. Americans were learning to live at the center of the stage of world politics; we were learning to live with the atomic bomb; we had to live with sputnik. In theology, neo-orthodoxy emphasized man's sinfulness and offered us in turn a high Christology.

It is not surprising that aestheticism hardly seemed sufficient to those distraught by postward anxieties. All around there was a search for more secure foundations. The "recovering our heritage" that flourished for a quarter century in worship now seems to have been a necessary and vital stage, though, I believe, one we have now gone beyond. We should not be surprised that two of the elements in worship that tended to be stressed were confession and creed. The fascination with confession was no accident; no one who lived through World War II could have much doubt about our sin. Professor Perry Miller once said he was an Emerson man till he led the tank corps that liberated Buchenwald; from then on he was a Jonathan Edwards man. Certainly we went to some excesses in stressing confession during this period, just as our predecessors had neglected it. And the creeds gave us something firm to stand on, a need we felt greatly.

We turned to the historians for more foundations. Bard Thompson's *Liturgies of the Western Church*[7] may well stand

---

[7](Cleveland: World, 1961.)

as the representative book of this period. It should be noticed that while he did pay homage to the ancient and medieval church, the great bulk of the book is devoted to Reformation liturgies and no space is given to the Eastern liturgies. This was characteristic of our interests at that time. We were rediscovering Bucer then, not Hippolytus. Presbyterians were reexamining Calvin and Knox, Methodists were beginning to recognize Wesley, and Lutherans were taking a new look at the early Lutheran *agendae.* Names such as W. D. Maxwell, J. E. Rattenbury, and Luther Reed stood out. The reformers were rediscovered with a bit of shock due to the belated realization of how much the nineteenth century had separated us from them.

The rediscovery of confession, with its emphasis on humanity's weakness, and the resurgence of the traditional creeds reflect the age of anxiety. Something was rattling the clouds overhead, and we had to find a substance in our worship that we had previously neglected.

But something totally new happened in the late 1960s and early 1970s to American culture, and we are beginning to see that it implied for our worship a new phase, that of pluralism. The cultural change involved a splintering of society. Whereas in the early 1960s we had a well-agreed image of what the good life in America consisted of, it would have been hard to find any unanimity on that by 1975. The conformity of the past with regard to life-styles, morality, proper dress, hair styles— almost anything you can name—was shattered in the late 1960s. We had moved into a period of diversity, pluralism, three-consciousnesses, or whatever label you use. This was not without shock and conflicts as old conformities came toppling down. The period of respectability had ended.

The cultural changes were reflected in worship by a move to a pluralistic approach, beginning about 1965. I would attribute most of the changes in worship to attempts to find forms that fitted the perceptual and expressive patterns natural to a wide variety of people. In this pluralistic approach to worship we rediscovered some of the things that revivalism knew. We needed to know and understand people in order to plan Christian worship. We needed to take seriously the importance of the whole body and all the senses in worship and to recognize that music was a body art. We needed to sense the importance of spontaneity and its advantages over a professionally conducted and controlled service as smooth as butter. Many so-called contemporary worship services seemed to appeal equally well both to the long-haired crowd and the gray-haired crowd.

We learned to recognize just how much our society was mixed. In almost every congregation there were "consciousness one" folks who wanted to sing the "old" hymns (i.e., those of revivalism), "consciousness two" people who wanted to sing the "good" hymns (i.e., those which are in good taste), and "consciousness three" persons who wanted to sing "something that moves" (i.e., those songs which had a "beat"). We realized that none of these was more Christian or more adequate than any of the others. We learned to think of our church music in terms of being "good for" whom, not in abstract terms of quality. Years ago when I fretted at a small-town congregation for not singing Ralph Vaughn Williams' "Sine nomine," I had not yet realized that what was good for a seminarian might not be good for California ranchers.

Church music often provides a good index. The fact that the new Lutheran communion service appeared in 1970 with four musical settings, as distinct as chant and folk song, was a sign of what we accomplished. The pluralistic approach came not without difficulties, but there was good precedent for being all things to all people in order to serve them well. The slogan of this period may well have been "serving everyone." This reflects, I hope, a broader tolerance, a more open society, a culture that moved a bit closer to mutual respect.

II

What can we conclude from this quick survey? Is Christ best served by abandoning the spirit and style of our culture? Or is he better served by mirroring the *Geist* of an age? Is our worship best seen as a mirror reflecting the bright light of its surroundings, or as a beacon shining in darkness? Obviously, we cannot give a clear yes to either alternative. With one we get a sentimental baptizing of the values of small-town America; with the other we have the dark obscurantism of Roman Catholic worship after Trent.

There remains a persistent tension between worship and culture in which worship both affirms and criticizes the culture with which it must live. I am convinced that Christian worship has functions and forms that are distinct from any given culture, yet adaptable to all. If Christian worship could survive nearly twenty centuries and exist in all parts of the world, surely it can adapt to many, if not all, cultures, yet be identified with none. There is, then, a constancy in Christian worship which is not culturally contingent, and yet a dependency upon culture in order to minister to people. We do have to speak a language, but what we say with it is for us to determine.

How do we avoid identifying worship with a particular cultural pattern, yet not be indifferent to the culture with which it must operate? I have tried to suggest one way already in this chapter—simply by being aware how extensively and subtly our culture affects the decisions we have to make about worship. The study of our history helps sensitize us to this problem.

A second possibility is by having a working definition of what we understand Christian worship to be. This gives us a place on which to stand, to see if we are being submerged by our culture or merely nourished by it. If we take the trouble to think through what we mean by Christian worship we shall find that we can be both detached from and involved in our culture. Then we do not run the risk of sacrificing something essential, yet we can avoid needless obscurantisms.

What, then, is Christian worship? I think we can begin with what happens first: we assemble. But assembly is far from enough, especially, as Paul warns us, if we fail to discern the body (I Cor. 11:29). The most obvious and yet easily missed fact about discerning the body is that it must be a common act, something done together. Yet the Corinthians missed this by not waiting for one another and by not considering one another. It may be that the most important single thing about worship is that it is done by the Christian assembly. We meet, assemble, come together, gather, congregate as those called out to assemble in Christ's name.

But the assembly for Christ has a purpose: *We come together, deliberately seeking to approach reality at its deepest level by becoming aware of God in and through Jesus Christ and by responding to this awareness.* Assembly with such a deliberate and communal expectation of awareness and response would seem to be normative for Christian worship, whatever the forms used may be. An occasion may be edifying, exciting, entertaining; but I would not deem it Christian worship unless the deliberate seeking, the awareness, and the response were present.[8]

There is another way of defining Christian worship. We have given a formal definition. But we can also give a material definition in which we pull together the constituent parts of Christian worship. There are certain basic and permanent structures of Christian worship that "at all times, and in all places" have remained constant. *These include the understanding and use of time as a means of communication, the*

---

[8]These concepts are developed in detail in chapters 2 and 3 of my *New Forms of Worship* (Nashville: Abingdon Press, 1971).

rites of Christian initiation, the Lord's Supper, and the divine office.

Frankly, I do not look for these four basic structures of Christian worship to be replaced. I look, instead, for them to continue to change in form as cultures change. These structures do not limit the possibilities open to us. To the contrary, they are spurs to our imagination to press on. The warm, folksy Lord's Supper of the revival period (often concluding the camp meeting with a harvest of all the converted) became the rich aesthetic experience of the 1920s (with special service music), only to become the historical exercise of the newly recovered reformers' liturgies (with prayers and garb from the sixteenth century), once again to become the youth mass of the 1970s (with improvised texts and guitar music). And these in turn will give way to further cultural development of forms.

Thus we seek awareness of the interplay of culture and Christian worship. The periods most to be feared are when they are too widely separated, as in the freeze of Roman Catholic liturgy after Trent or the lethargy of much Protestant worship in many parts of the world today. As long as the church has a clear formal and material concept of its worship, it is free to relate to varying cultures. The church has much to gain as it welcomes cultural change to its worship and much to give to changing culture itself. Once we have a firm grasp of the basic structures of Christian worship, we are free to relate in new and creative ways to changing cultural patterns. We who are perfectly captive are also perfectly free through Jesus Christ.

V

Individuality and Liturgy

Most of the history of worship is anonymous. Practices devoid of the names of originators simply appeared at times and places, difficult to date and locate precisely. It is the exception to find the name of an individual as the instigator of a new liturgical custom. For the most part, we can simply trace a series of developments that affect the worship of the Christian people without being able to praise or to blame individual originators. The history of Christian worship is mainly a nameless and faceless history.

Histories of worship read quite differently from histories of doctrine, where ideas are almost always identified by author. Doctrines are neatly labeled "Augustinian," "Thomistic," "Zwinglian," etc., to distinguish the varying contributions of individuals. Apparently theological ideas are more traceable than liturgical practices. Personal labels mark doctrines; anonymity masks worship practices.

Much of the origins of Christian worship, of course, is hidden in the obscurity of early church history. Even some of the names we do have are pseudonyms such as those for liturgies named after saints associated with various localities: Mark, James, Addai and Mari, Basil, Chrysostom, and Peter.

Much of the obscurity is no doubt intentional. A case in point is the recent Consilium for the Implementation of the Constitution on the Sacred Liturgy. Even the list of those who did the actual work of liturgical revision was published *sub secreto*. I was only able to borrow it during a lunch hour from a Roman Catholic friend. Protestant liturgical commissions operate with similar anonymity but less secrecy. In both cases speculation and gossip often identify who was responsible for what.

There are good reasons for the anonymity of worship commissions. A liturgical document for the use of the whole church ought to be refined and revised by trial use and reflect polishing by many hands. We hope that through this process the contributions of individuals get assimilated into a product superior to its separate ingredients. The work of councils, commissions, and committees, we trust, profits from the sharing and cross-fertilization of representatives of differing perspectives and backgrounds. It is hoped that the resulting products have a universality and breadth which serve well the greatest possible variety of Christians. Much of the history of Christian worship, then, is made by anonymous committees who select texts and music for hymnals, collect prayers, compile lectionaries, and do the thousand chores that produce liturgical books. I shall examine this process in the chapter following this one. At this point, I merely suggest that worship committees, both past and present, have probably worked best in anonymity.

Occasionally though, at unexpected times and places in history, the mists of impersonality lift and we can glimpse the unique contribution of a single individual to making worship happen. Then we can cite a name and say "this is the person who put it there." I shall note a few of these rare individuals whose names and work both remain, looming like islands above the flat surface of the surrounding waters. Perhaps this can give us some present guidance in discussing the relative values of personal vs. anonymous liturgy. At least it may make us aware of individual roles in the shaping of worship.

Recent years have seen much discussion and conflict between the private and personal liturgical productions of individuals and the official formularies of the churches. What is the role of the liturgical contributions of a few gifted individuals (and many not so gifted)? What part, on the other hand, do the publications and pronouncements of denominational and ecumenical agencies play? How much ought worship to be colored by the idiosyncrasies of creative personalities? Ought we to prefer the consensus of the faithful as expressed by official commissions on worship?

My purpose in this reflection is to give a bit of historical perspective on these questions by examining the relationship of individual personalities and the public liturgy of the church. I shall briefly characterize the work of twenty identifiable shapers of worship, mostly confining my attention to Western Christianity. I shall also mention in passing an equal number of lesser lights. Certainly not everyone would agree that these are the chief personalities who made liturgy or even that their contributions were positive ones. But I think these people are all of major significance and trust that cataloging them may cause others to reflect on the varying roles of individuals in making liturgy.

I

It is difficult to decide whether to list Hippolytus under the third century or the twentieth. His claim to liturgical fame is that he stimulated change in the latter by resisting it in the former. But then Hippolytus is a man of contradictions, the only anti-pope to be canonized. His *Apostolic Tradition* was the work of a conservative, determined to prevent experimentation in worship. Yet in our time his stubborn clinging to old ways has prompted new forms: concelebration, a replacement for the Roman canon, parts of several new Protestant eucharistic liturgies, revisions of the ordinal, and major changes in the process of Christian initiation. Much of Hippolytus' influence came through documents which did not bear his name. It was only in the twentieth century that his most important work was identified and not until after Vatican II that he showed the way forward to a post-Constantinian Christianity by his witness back to pre-Constantinian worship.

Certainly no one's actions have affected Christian worship,

both directly and indirectly, as much as those of the emperor Constantine. Most obvious was his decision "to give Christians and all others liberty to follow whatever form of worship they choose." Henceforth Christian worship became public, performed without fear of persecution. The consequences of becoming respectable were tremendous and amounted to a major revolution in the whole style of worship. It meant, as Dix said,[1] that Christians "became reconciled to *time*," and worship shifted its focus from looking ahead to Christ's second coming to recalling his incarnation. Constantine did much to change the setting of worship by building magnificent basilicas in Rome, Constantinople, Nicomedia, Antioch, Tyre, and many other cities. Aided by his mother, Helena, he built churches in Bethlehem, on the Mount of Olives, and at the Holy Sepulchre. Of the latter, he decreed, "Not only shall this basilica be the finest in the world, but . . . the details also shall be such that all the fairest structures in every city may be surpassed by it." Furnishings and endowments were lavished on new churches. It was a far cry from the days of persecuted Christians, worshiping privately in their homes, to gatherings of multitudes, surrounded by such imperial splendor. Christian worship has never since been the same. Ironically, these changes were all made before Constantine was baptized into the church.

The Constantinian world at worship is represented by our next individual, Cyril, Bishop of Jerusalem during the latter half of the fourth century. Some innovations of that time and place may be due to others, but Cyril is usually credited. Whoever it was, he certainly had a profound understanding of how time and place can be used as means of communication in Christian worship. It was an insight thoroughly in accord with the Jewish understanding of worship. As Bishop of Jerusalem, Cyril presided over the sites of the climactic events in the life

---

[1]*Shape of the Liturgy* (Westminster: Dacre Press, 1945), p. 305.

of Christ. He did what any good Chamber of Commerce would do: if you live in Winter Haven, Florida, you have a citrus festival; in St. Albans, Vermont, a maple sugar festival. In Jerusalem, you put time and place together and develop a series of services centering in the triumphant entry, last supper, death, and resurrection of the Lord. The result is the drama of Holy Week and the Jerusalem celebrations at the Constantinian churches. Egeria described these services for the benefit of the ladies back home, and the Jerusalem observances soon became universal. Cyril is remembered, too, for his catechetical lectures, as was his contemporary Ambrose also known for his hymnody.

Abbot Suger was not an architect, but he played a crucial role in the development of Gothic architecture and was an ardent promoter of the visual arts in worship. In the first half of the twelfth century, Suger had the opportunity to begin a major rebuilding of the royal abbey of St. Denis in Paris. The building still stands, a magnificent monument in itself. More important, though, was Suger's combination of the light mysticism of Pseudo-Dionysius with his own love of the arts. This helped him provide a philosophical basis for Gothic, the architecture of light. In the rebuilding of the apse at St. Denis, Gothic first happened. Certainly it must be regarded as a triumph of engineering as well as theology, but never have the two been so closely fused. The advent of Gothic introduced a whole new visual and acoustical environment for Christian worship. For better or for worse, monastic churches were the pacesetters and for centuries influenced the design and construction of cathedral and parish churches as well.

In recent years we have learned how important is the interpretation of Christian worship. A thirteenth-century writer, Bishop William Durandus, was the preeminent interpreter of Christian worship for three whole centuries. Durandus was Bishop of Mende in southern France, though he worked in Rome, visiting his diocese only during the last five years of his life. His chief contribution, the *Rationale Divinorum Officiorum*, was the textbook on worship for centuries. Though others, from Amalar of Metz onward, had written explanations of Christian worship, Durandus outdid them all both in thoroughness and in popularity. The *Rationale* was the fifth book to be printed and ran through forty-four editions in the fifteenth century alone (as compared to nineteen for Augustine's *City of God*). Rarely have liturgical commentators been such best sellers! Yet after the fifty-ninth edition in 1614 the *Rationale* quietly disappeared for 229 years. Durandus' purpose in the *Rationale* was continuing education. As he says: "Priests and bishops . . . in these days . . . apprehend but little of those things which day by day they handle and perform, what they signify, and wherefore they were instituted." He had a splendid imagination in supplying this lack, and the volume contains fanciful, symbolic explanations of every item and action used in worship. Durandus stands out as the most significant interpreter of Western Christian worship in history. In the East the writings of Nicolas Cabasilas served a somewhat similar function. Mention should also be made of Durandus' pontifical, which came to rival and influence its Roman prototype.

The Reformation brings us to a different era, an age of individualism in liturgical writing as in so many other ways. Martin Luther took the leadership in ways that affected all subsequent Protestant worship. In the five crucial years for Protestant liturgies, 1522–26, Luther's work was second to none in importance. He essayed masses in 1523 (Latin) and 1526 (German). Luther was not the first to put the mass into the vernacular. Diobald Schwarz did so in 1524, preceded by Kaspar Kantz (1522) and Thomas Müntzer (1523).

Luther's contemporary, Ulrich Zwingli, came at reform from the perspective of a humanist. In his reform, most of the ceremonial which Luther tolerated, if not approved, disappeared. Zwingli's liturgical ideas took shape in *Action or Use of the Lord's Supper*, 1525.

Except for Luther, it is hard to imagine anyone else whose influence was as widespread as Martin Bucer's. As pastor in Strasbourg during Calvin's exile there, Bucer influenced the Reformed tradition through his revision of the Roman mass. Free Churchmen knew Bucer through Calvin's borrowing and Anglicans through his friendship with Archbishop Cranmer and impact on the second prayer book.

John Calvin wanted communion weekly but was thwarted by local politicians. In 1542 Calvin produced his *Form of Church Prayers According to the Custom of the Ancient Church*, based on the work of his predecessor in Geneva, Guillaume Farel, and his associate in Strasbourg, Bucer. Through John Knox, worship in the Church of Scotland and in all Presbyterianism was shaped by Calvin's work.

Archbishop Thomas Cranmer brought many advantages to liturgical writing. He could draw with equal ease from the work of Catholic and Protestant antagonists in the attempted reform in Cologne and was very receptive to the reforming work of Cardinal Francesco de Quiñones. Cranmer was the master of English liturgical prose, perhaps too much so. G. B. Shaw once said that Shakespeare had ruined English drama for subsequent playwrights, and one sometimes suspects that Cranmer did the same for those who would write English liturgies. He succeeded in reordering and compressing the multitude of clerical service books into a single volume of truly common prayer. In doing this, he applied the new print medium more successfully than any of his predecessors.

No one could be more different from the scholarly archbishop than George Fox, founder of the Quakers. In many ways, Fox was the most radical of all the reformers. Cranmer reduced the service books to one; Fox eliminated even that, substituting a quiet waiting upon God in which people stand aside and let the Spirit speak when and as it pleases.

We cannot ignore the work of architects in changing Christian worship. Sir Christopher Wren was as influential as anyone in shaping the physical environment of Protestant worship. During the first century after the Reformation, Protestants largely reordered existing buildings, while Catholics developed the possibilities of baroque. The great fire of 1666 gave Wren the opportunity to build scores of churches in London, and he did so on the basis that they should "be fitted for Auditories." Wren developed for Protestant worship the auditory church, a single-volume building devoid of chancels and side chapels. He did for space what others had done for service books. The classical fashion with which he clothed his space, however elegant, is less significant than his original and successful effort to organize space specifically for worship according to the *Book of Common Prayer*.

English-speaking Protestantism remains heavily indebted to Isaac Watts, an Independent (Congregationalist) minister. Unlike Lutherans and Anabaptists, English Protestants had avoided nonscriptural hymnody as human invention and preferred worship based only on inspired texts. Watts more than anyone else helped to overcome this rigid biblicism that bound the worship of the English Free Churches. He began with the metrical psalm paraphrases that then prevailed, trying to make David sing like a Christian. But Watts moved to things David never imagined, such as "When I Survey the Wondrous Cross" or "Alas! and Did My Savior Bleed." It is often said that hymnody became the Nonconformist contribution to Christian worship and more than made up for lack of service books. Watts led the way, and his hymns are an intensely personal contribution of his own individual piety to corporate worship.

We would not want to neglect church musicians. I have chosen J. S. Bach to represent these people, not because he stands alone but because he is so eminent and such a large portion of his composition was for use in worship. Painters, sculptors, and other artists have contributed to Christian worship, but their influence has tended to be local; music is portable. Bach's greatness lies not as much in the creation of new forms as in making it possible for people to praise God magnificently through organ and choral works. Moved by a strong stream of Pietism, Bach wrote compositions that are both deeply personal and highly abstract, almost mathematical in intellectual clarity. The role Luther saw for church music was fulfilled and more in Bach, who brought service music to a new splendor.

John and Charles Wesley left their imprint on Christian worship, not simply as founders of Methodism but as writers of a flood of hymnody that flowed throughout Christendom. John Wesley was a catholic person, putting his patristic scholarship to work in a pragmatic way to fit the particular needs of his place and time. He succeeded in fusing a rich, sacramental Christianity with a fervent evangelicalism as few have been able to do since.

John Mason Neale was also a great hymn writer, but his contributions lie in a variety of other directions as well. Neale led the nineteenth-century Cambridge Movement in its efforts to return the Church of England to the forms of medieval worship. More than any other individual, Neale led the way to reversing the work of the Reformation and the Enlightenment by returning to the splendors, outward and visible, of the early fourteenth century. That was, for him, the golden age of worship. Churches were once again to be Gothic, have long and distinct chancels, and be embellished with all the arts. Neale helped inaugurate the restoration of religious communities, vestments, and a host of ceremonial forms disused since the Reformation. A brilliant scholar, Neale enlisted Durandus to teach the need for symbolism in church architecture and helped change Anglican church building for a century. Much effort in our time has gone into undoing what Neale and his colleagues accomplished so successfully. What was right in his time seems wrong in ours. One thing remains unchallenged, though—the treasury of medieval hymns Neale translated and recovered for modern use. "Jerusalem the Golden," "O Come, O Come, Emmanuel," and "All Glory, Laud, and Honor" are ours today because of his research and translations. Neale's work was paralleled in some ways by that of Dom Prosper Guéranger in France and in the efforts of Edward Irving for the Catholic Apostolic Church. We should also mention the opposite stream in worship, American revivalism, which Charles G. Finney personified so well. Both movements meant a recovery of feeling and emotion in worship, but otherwise their styles were about as different as could be.

I have not included papal names, whatever the personal contributions of Gregory I, Leo I, and Gelasius I may have been. We cannot, though, overlook Pius X, who made respectable new (or very old) directions in Catholic worship through his stress on the whole people of God praying the mass. It is easily forgotten how recent frequent communion has been for Roman Catholics, so widespread has it become since early in this century. Pius X must also be remembered for his influence on music in parish churches. Scholars will debate how much genuine interest Pius XII had in liturgical reform, though his *Mediator Dei* gave a grudging acceptance, if not leadership.

The real hero of the liturgical movement was a Belgian Benedictine monk, Lambert Beauduin. At last he has been recognized as one of the great prophetic figures of our time. If the liturgical movement had a father, it was he; if it had a birthday, it could well have been a talk he gave in 1909. His tireless career of teaching, writing, and influencing other people contributed to changes in the whole western church, culminating in the *Constitution on the Sacred Liturgy*. In a sense, Beauduin had spent fifty years in preparing for this document, though he did not live to see the Council begin.

Beauduin is also noted as a pioneer ecumenist and founded a monastery at Chevetogne, Belgium, uniting both Western and Eastern rites. His influence was contagious, and other great leaders such as the American Benedictine Virgil Michel engaged in an apostolate of publicizing a new understanding of the role of liturgy in the life of Christians. A. G. Hebert mediated Beauduin's ideas within the Church of England.

I do not know whether Gregory Dix ever participated in the work of a committee engaged in writing liturgy or not. I rather doubt it since his most active years lay between the liturgy-writing epochs of the 1920s and the 1960s. Yet his influence has been present in every committee engaged in preparing eucharistic texts ever since that of the Church of South India. His book *The Shape of the Liturgy* has helped us realize the role of action in worship. Dix represents the culmination of a great series of English liturgical scholars, especially Bishop W. H. Frere.

A scholar of equal influence was Josef A. Jungmann, S.J., who stood at the forefront of a great tradition of historical scholarship in Germanic lands. Basically conservative, Jungmann became a powerful change agent in his clear analysis of what had gone wrong in the liturgy through the course of history. His careful portrait of the history of the mass shows how important a tool historical studies can be in pastoral efforts. Jungmann eased the way for many of the changes made since Vatican II by making the Church conscious of much it had lost or misvalued. He also gave a profound impetus to liturgical studies in our time.

II

Can any conclusions be drawn from this admittedly subjective collection of capsule liturgical biographies? A few observations suggest themselves. For one thing, I am struck by the limited range of those who are identifiable as having made contributions to the liturgy. With the exception of the artists and Constantine they are all clergy, though George Fox would not relish the term. Several were bishops (Cyril, Durandus, and Cranmer); some were monastics (Suger, Beauduin, and Dix). With few exceptions, most were scholars and all (except the artists) were writers, ranging from Fox's humble *Journal* to Pius X's *Motu proprio*. It is significant that none were women, thus neatly eliminating half the body of Christ. Indeed, in twenty centuries I could not discover any female names more distinguished than Helena and hymn writers Fanny J. Crosby or Julia Ward Howe. Clericalism and sexism, then, form important perimeters. Thus the visible creative work throughout church history has been done by a small, male, clerical minority. That may very well be true of the present time, too, when one tries to find female and lay counterparts to such names as Oosterhuis, Hoey, and Gallen. Such an unrepresentative situation is not desirable.

Second, we cannot help observing the immense variety of ways in which individuals have made their own personal contributions to the liturgy. I tried to show how disparate the talents of these differing personalities have been and how distinct and precious the efforts of each proved to be. Committee work simply cannot produce a Durandus or a Fox; their talents are unique. This ought to be realized today in determining the place of people such as Oosterhuis or Maertens. But it ought also to be remembered that most of the men described above made their contributions through means other than the writing of liturgical texts. The Reformation was the exception, though the situation today may be similar.

In the third place, I think we can see in these men people who recognized a need for some kind of change and helped effect it. They were all, though in differing ways, change agents. Some, such as Hippolytus or Durandus, probably did not desire that but brought it about nevertheless. It is striking how much change has been accomplished by instructing people in the meaning of liturgy both in the thirteenth century and the twentieth. This would reinforce the importance of the publicist in the life of the church, a role historians often neglect.

Finally, I think we can see the great importance of individual contributions rich with the distinct flavor of the personality involved. But these gifts have little significance until merged with the anonymous tradition of the whole church. The individual and the anonymous make Christian worship happen. Thus we need the *editio typica,* but we also must have the paperback service book printed for a local community guided by a gifted person. It would be a supreme misfortune for us to think that we must choose between either one. I hope my list of remembered individuals has shown how vital the work of distinct individuals has been in the development of Christian worship and yet how readily really significant work has been absorbed into the anonymous, ongoing tradition.

Individuality and anonymity have worked together in partnership despite occasional conflicts. If we had to rely only on those developments traceable to known individuals, the history of Christian worship would be brief indeed. Yet without these people it would be a dull account. Fortunately their distinct personal contributions blend into the faceless and nameless anonymity to give it spice and flavor; yet their work is itself enriched by tradition. Our problem, then, seems to be that of provoking more personal contributions from a wider segment of the church, particularly those majorities from whom we have not heard. They in turn need patterns of excellence to keep them faithful to the central life of the whole community of Christ.

VI

Inside the Liturgical Establishment

There is a liturgical establishment that makes the basic liturgical decisions for most American Christians. This liturgical establishment serves approximately eighty million of America's roughly one hundred thirty million Christians and, directly or indirectly, many millions more overseas. I intend to interpret and evaluate the processes through which the liturgical establishment works for American Christians.

Essentially the liturgical establishment consists of nine denominational and ecumenical agencies: the Roman Catholic Church's Congregation for the Sacraments and Divine Worship (and its international and national affiliates), the Standing Liturgical Commission of the Episcopal Church, the Section on Worship of the Board of Discipleship of The United Methodist Church, the Commission on Worship of the United Church of Christ, the Christian Church (Disciples of Christ) worship leadership, the Presbyterian Joint Committee on Worship, the Inter-Lutheran Commission on Worship, the Commission on Worship of the Consultation on Church Union, and the International Consultation on English Texts. In addition, there are a number of unofficial organizations and publications that operate on the periphery of the establishment, often being scarcely distinguishable from it.

It is true, of course, that there are many American Christians whose worship life has not been affected by these agencies. Most of them belong to the denominations, both large and small, which have no central organization. The Baptists are the most numerous of these Christian people, but a wide variety of other churches operate without much centralized assistance for congregations in the area of worship.

Most of these churches fall in either the Free Church tradition or the Pentecostal. Except for the Quakers, most parts of other Protestant traditions (Lutheran, Reformed, Anglican, and Methodist) operate quite comfortably with a centralized worship establishment.

Within denominations heavily committed to the liturgical establishment there are segments not served by it. No part of the establishment has produced a marriage service for homosexuals. There are conservatives in the Episcopal Church who resent any attempt at prayerbook revision. Even more numerous may be avant-garde congregations which find their denomination's liturgical revision does not go far or fast enough. Like Free Church people of another era, they want to cast off the dregs of the past and press on to something more authentic for them. Thus there are elements within each denomination that feel themselves ignored by the establishment. Sometimes this is due to problems in communication. It is not uncommon for a local church to discover a service its denominational worship commission put out years before. On other occasions, the commission finds it underestimated the acceptance its work would have.

There is, then, a sizable segment of American Christianity, both outside and within the denominations with centralized liturgical agencies, that is not affected by the establishment. It is very easy to ignore these people in writing about worship today, even though they number over fifty million, because they lack the visibility that publications and conferences give the establishment types. Who can tell what transitions Baptist worship is undergoing except by interviewing people from hundreds of congregations? And thus by default it is easy to ignore transitions among Baptists, however significant these changes may be.

My present purpose is to show the processes by which the liturgical establishment works for its constituents and to comment on the successes and failures of such processes. I propose only to give a quick overview and I am sure there are omissions. I shall avoid naming individuals, though much credit should go to many persons who have given generously of themselves to help others worship. My concern, then, is with the process, not the personalities or products. I shall deal mainly with the ten years from 1966 through 1975.

A natural question is: Is the establishment where real liturgical creativity occurs? This chapter should be read in connection with chapter 5 on individual creativity. I hope it will be apparent that there is much interaction between the anonymous liturgical creativity reflected in the liturgical establishment (discussed here) and the contributions of individuals (described in chapter 5).

I

The most impressive array of resources and talents ever devoted to liturgical reform has been that amassed by the Roman Catholic Church since Vatican II. So massive has the work been that it has had to be carried out at three levels: worldwide, international, and national. I can only suggest here the overall process, but it is important to grasp the magnitude and quality of the resources that the Roman Catholic Church considered the work to merit. For example, when Protestant groups revise a lectionary, it usually ends up as the spare-time work of a busy individual with a few hours of public sessions devoted to reviewing his or her work. The Roman Catholic Church was able to place a priest in charge of this work, give him several years of full-time labor to get on with it, and allow him opportunity to reach out to some eight hundred consultants. In this particular case, we have all been beneficiaries. The Roman Catholic Church placed a very high priority on liturgical reform in the allocation of its resources. All too often, Protestant churches have been known to commit a million dollars to other purposes while begrudging a few thousands for worship renewal.

Modern liturgical change in the Roman Catholic Church was formally initiated by the promulgation of the *Constitution on the Sacred Liturgy* by Pope Paul VI on December 4, 1963, though crucial work had been done before the Council by the Preparatory Commission. The first stage was the formation of the Consilium for the Implementation of the Constitution on the Sacred Liturgy (known as the Consilium) which soon began operation. The first plenary session was held on March 11, 1964, and three others followed within the same year. The first significant event occurred on September 26, 1964, when the Congregation of Sacred Rites (in existence since the sixteenth century) issued its *Instruction for the Proper Implementation of the Constitution on the Sacred Liturgy*, eventually known as the "first" instruction. Another followed on May 4, 1967. These gave guidance to the first stages of liturgical reform, especially those items that the Council had mandated and that could be instituted before revision of the liturgical books was complete.

This revision became the chief function of the Consilium. It functioned as a body of bishops from all parts of the world, gathering in Rome for roughly semiannual sessions to make decisions on the revisions. The actual work of revising the liturgical books—breviary, missal, pontifical, ritual, martyrology, musical books, episcopal ceremonial, even the rites of the papal chapel—was broken up and each segment assigned to a *coetus* of liturgical experts which met more frequently. They, in turn, were assisted by various consultors. The Consilium maintained an office inside the Vatican City, almost in the shadow of the sacristy of St. Peter's. Staff persons there coordinated efforts of the various *coetus*, received reports on material in use *ad experimentum*, and worked toward the publication of completed efforts.

The addition of non-Catholic observers to the sessions of the Consilium in 1966 was a significant step. To recent criticisms of ultraconservative Catholics that the presence of these non-Catholic observers affected Catholic revision, Archbishop Bugnini (former secretary of the Congregation for Divine Worship) exploded: *"Niente da niente!"* (loosely translated: "baloney!"). The non-Catholic observers, however, were consulted about the lectionary and other matters and their advice taken seriously. Their presence was a fact unthinkable for four hundred years and an indication of steps that would lead to real ecumenical cooperation before the decade was ended.

Some indication of the magnitude of the task attempted is shown by the fact that the work of liturgical revision continued ten years after Vatican II. The Consilium itself became a part of the Congregation for Divine Worship in 1969, renamed in 1975 the Congregation for the Sacraments and Divine Worship. In the meantime, hundreds of meetings of the *coetus* have been held, countless drafts submitted, used, revised, and decisions made on their acceptability by the Consilium. Once approved, texts are reviewed by the Pope and finally issued under his authority by the Congregation. The text then appears in a Latin *editio typica*, and the work for the universal Church has been done. A very useful publication, *Notitiae* (Libreria Editrice Vaticana, Vatican City), was begun in January, 1965. Published monthly, with different sections in Latin, Italian, Spanish, French, or English, it gives an overview of decisions, interpretations, and official liturgical publications of the Roman curia.

Once an *editio typica* has been released by the Roman Congregation, it is still a long time before the service can be used on Main Street, U.S.A. It then goes to international commissions for the English-, French-, German-, and Spanish-speaking nations and many others. Our concern is with the International Commission on English in the Liturgy. The ICEL is composed of an episcopal board representing each English-speaking nation, an advisory board, and a secretariat (1330 Massachusetts Ave., N.W., Washington,

D.C. 20005). The ICEL is charged with producing English translations for eleven English-speaking nations. The Secretariat of the ICEL (which has included both clerical and lay experts as its head) farms out the translations of the *editio typica* to individuals and committees for the actual work of translation, which then goes to the Advisory Committee, composed of priests, religious, and laity. A "green book" draft translation is then submitted for consultation to all the bishops of the English-speaking world. Their comments are reviewed, and then, by a two-thirds majority, the Episcopal Board approves the final "white book" translation. After confirmation by Rome and approval of a national conference of bishops, the white book is submitted to commercial publishers.

Of course, the stage of translation is not usually necessary for Protestant denominations. Nevertheless we have all profited from the work of the ICEL. The ICEL led the way in producing modern English liturgical prose. Since it was working from Latin texts, it did not have the problem of modernizing Elizabethan English but could approach the subject with a freedom unknown to Protestants. In its early years, the ICEL was subject to some suspicion on the part of heresy hunters who detected dangers in the handling of phrases felicitous in Latin but infeasible in English. The ICEL did serious study of the liturgical use of English and, though the results were much more inconclusive than hoped for, the example of the ICEL's translation has helped to liberate us all. In 1974 the ICEL began the publication of a *Newsletter*.

Even this international-level work does not bring the results to Main Street. National episcopal conferences still can accept or reject the work of the ICEL. Other matters such as the manner of the distribution of communion (hand or mouth) are made on the national (or regional) level, subject to Rome's review. In this country, the Bishops' Committee on the Liturgy helps formulate policy, subject to the review of all the bishops in the National Conference of Catholic Bishops.

Since 1965 the Bishops' Committee on the Liturgy (1312 Massachusetts Ave., N.W., Washington, D.C. 20005) has published a monthly *Newsletter*. This provides a very useful means of communication with diocesan liturgical commissions and others interested in knowing what are the latest liturgical developments. There is also a semi-official Federation of Diocesan Liturgical Commissions. Some dioceses, such as Chicago, have well-staffed liturgical commissions which communicate directly with local parishes. After passing through all these filters, what began in Rome passes in all its purity to the local parish. It is not surprising that some parishes have been impatient and taken matters into their own hands. Protestants, being accustomed only to the national level of decision-making, tend to operate independently of churches overseas. Consequently, Episcopalians and Lutherans diverge from the lectionaries adopted by their parents overseas. The National Office for Black Catholics (1234 Massachusetts Ave. NW, Washington, D.C. 20005) also publishes materials regarding worship.

Despite the complexity of the Catholic liturgical establishment, the chains of communication are remarkably clear, and it is quite possible to keep up with every level of activity by subscribing to the proper periodicals. Indeed, one can have the feeling of being better informed about Roman Catholic efforts than of those within his own denomination. The value of such communication is hard to overlook. The chief defects of the Roman Catholic method of liturgical reform would seem to be over-centralization (each significant variance demands a decree from Rome), over-clericalization (the experts in Rome are all clerical, and the national decisions are made only by bishops), and over-lengthy process so that items of value may be lost by the impatient (as with the liturgy of the hours). Still, both the quantity and the quality of the work accomplished must impress any observer. It is to be hoped that revision of the liturgical books will soon be complete and local cultural adaptation can come to the forefront.

In the Episcopal Church the process of liturgical reform has been persistent and thorough, though hardly encouraging to the impatient. Whereas Rome cranked up its liturgical establishment after Vatican II, the Episcopal Church has been in this process for over a quarter of a century. Action on revision of the present American *Book of Common Prayer* ended in 1925. The 1949 General Convention authorized the Standing Liturgical Commission to publish its findings on fresh revision. It began this in 1950, noting in Volume I of *Prayer Book Studies* that "there is a widespread and insistent demand for a general revision of the Prayer Book." In 1964 trial use of approved new material was made possible. With a bit of luck, the action of the 1949 General Convention should bear fruit in 1979 in the publication of the fourth American *Book of Common Prayer*. Episcopalians are not to be rushed. In a full generation some concepts have had time to mature, and others have been outgrown. We now stand at *Prayer Book Studies 28* and holding. Meanwhile, the *Studies* have not only chronicled changes but contributed considerably to liturgical knowledge. Other churches have often had to learn the hard way the pitfalls of skipping such "position paper" studies.

The Standing Liturgical Commission consists of bishops, priests, and a few lay people. Most of its work is done by individual drafting committees which submit their work to the full SLC for review. The results ultimately go to the General Convention of the Episcopal Church for approval or rejection. The SLC has done excellent work in using a wide variety of consultors from both the Episcopal Church and other denominations. Mail from them now stacks nine inches high in my office. A thorough job has been done in sampling and evaluating the reactions of significant numbers of lay people as revisions are proposed.

One cannot understand the Episcopal situation without

considering the love affair of Episcopalians with "our incomparable liturgy." There is no real parallel situation with other churches. So intense has feeling been about retention of the 1928 prayer book that the Society to Preserve the Book of Common Prayer retained public relations personnel to campaign before the 1973 General Convention. Nevertheless that Convention voted heavily in favor of continued work on revision. It is encouraging that in one church, at least, liturgical questions could be taken seriously enough to cause such a struggle on the floor of the national church assembly. Constitutional safeguards abound so that the proposed prayer book, if accepted in 1976, still must await further approval in 1979. By that time many Protestant groups may well be into second- or third-generation liturgies.

The most significant accomplishments thus far include the publication of *Prayer Book Studies XVII: The Liturgy of the Lord's Supper* in 1966 and *PBS 18: Holy Baptism with the Laying-on-of-Hands* (1970). These gave way, in turn, to *Services for Trial Use*, authorized in 1970; *Authorized Services, 1973;* and *The Draft Proposed Book of Common Prayer* of 1976. A distinctive element has been the provision of both traditional and contemporary-language versions of the eucharist, morning and evening prayers, and the collects. Congregations thus can have the choice of retaining traditional language but in services whose structure has been considerably revamped. Four eucharistic prayers are available for the contemporary eucharist. An *ordo* is also provided with the possibility of improvisation in either of its eucharistic prayers. Thus Episcopalians can now go down both sides of the road and maybe even a bit on the left shoulder, although loyalty to the official text seems to be more characteristic of Episcopalians than of members of other churches. Hard questions have been asked about the process of Christian initiation. Only time will tell whether the current retreat to a more conventional mode, with baptism and confirmation once again treated as distinct events, represents a lost opportunity for liturgical progress.

The Episcopal Church operates without a worship executive as such. The nearest equivalent is the Coordinator for Prayer Book Revision (815 Second Ave., New York, N.Y. 10017).

One must respect the thoroughness of the Episcopal process of revision and the great investment it has meant in the print medium. On the other hand, one cannot but think that the ordinary Episcopal layman is less than enthusiastic about the whole affair and may take a while to learn the value of the old materials recovered and new possibilities gained. There seems to be no great pressure to revise the 1940 *Hymnal*. Maybe liturgics has gone a bit ahead of catechetics in the Episcopal Church.

The liturgical situation of The United Methodist Church is about as different as can be imagined. In liturgical reform much depends on the timing. History played a nasty trick on the Methodists. At the end of 1963, the Commission on Worship of the Methodist Church wrapped up its work on new editions of *The Methodist Hymnal* and *The Book of Worship*, replacing books published previously in 1935 and 1944. At almost the same moment, the *Constitution on the Sacred Liturgy* was being promulgated in Rome, opening up a whole new era of liturgical change. The new Methodist *Book of Worship* (1965) proved to be the last monument of an era that had just passed. The language was Cranmerian, and the view of history tended to reflect the Reformation rather than either the early church or new breakthroughs.

With this work behind itself, the Commission turned to catechetics. It embarked on the publishing of a *Companion to the Book of Worship* and a *Companion to the Hymnal*, work which moved slowly to publication in 1970. By that time, of course, we were in a whole new ball game; and the *Companion to the Book of Worship*, though still valuable, never did have the use it could have received if published earlier.

During the years 1964–1972, the Commission on Worship operated under the chairmanship of a bishop with a membership of ministers and lay people from each jurisdiction of the Church. There was no staff, though two dedicated individuals carried heavy responsibilities in their spare time while serving parishes full time. Consultants were also heavily involved in the meetings and work. Unlike the Commission members, the consultants were not restricted to eight years of service. Beginning in 1968 some staff help from within the Board of Evangelism became available.

A wholesale restructuring of United Methodist agencies in 1972 brought about permanent staffing through a new Section on Worship of the Board of Discipleship (Box 840, Nashville, TN 37202). Such full-time service has opened up many new possibilities and has been a tremendous enabling force.

In 1968 a project was initiated in connection with the Board of Evangelism to collect and publish various free-lance liturgical materials which, by that time, were at flood tide. This led to several publications between 1969 and 1973: *Ventures in Worship, Ventures in Worship 2, Ventures in Worship 3, Ventures in Song,* and a summary volume, *God's Party* (1975).

Another route was engendered within the Commission on Worship in 1970 as the Alternate Rituals Project. A task force of the Commission began work in 1970 on the first assignment, a contemporary communion service. After going through eight revisions and much testing, it was published as *The Sacrament of the Lord's Supper, An Alternate Text, 1972.* The response has surprised everyone; while intended to serve chiefly those congregations restless for change, it has been widely accepted and sold more than a million copies in the first four years it was available.

Buoyed up by this success, the Alternate Rituals Project was continued under the new Section on Worship. Procedural matters were tightened up with staff available and, profiting from previous mistakes, the Project made position papers rather than rites the point of departure. In 1974 a new calendar and three-year lectionary were produced through cooperation with the COCU Commission on Worship. A very significant development in the thought and practice of Christian initiation is reflected in *A Service of Baptism, Confirmation, and Renewal: An Alternate Text 1976*. Further down the road lie new services for marriages and funerals. A task force on the cultural context of ritual proposes, in *Ritual in a New Day: An Invitation,* some new types of services— e.g., services for endings and beginnings, for naming and foot washing, and for the dying. Accessory materials for a new basic pattern of Sunday worship are in *Word and Table*. Eventually all these new materials may be collected in a single volume, or they may simply be replaced by second- and third-generation services. This piecemeal publication process has some advantages, but it also discourages investment in good graphic design and printing, the composition of service music, and the preparation of educational materials.

Methodists do not seem to have solved the problem of communications. It is not uncommon to find pastors who are unaware of the 1972 communion service. With the collapse of denominational publications, it becomes ever more difficult to educate clergy and laity to proposed changes, especially those as far-reaching as recent changes in the initiation process. The problem is not opposition to change but the absence of information as to the historical, theological, and pastoral reasons for such changes. National convocations on worship have been held in 1966, 1969, and 1975. These reach some people, and commissions on worship in the annual conferences help more. Some of these conference commissions have actively promoted workshops and publications on worship for years; others have hardly explored their potential. In 1975 a United Methodist Society for Worship was formed which may come to be as effective as the Fellowship of United Methodist

Musicians has been. The Order of St. Luke is a liturgical society dating from 1948.

Time served the United Church of Christ better. Indeed the denomination itself presented a fresh opportunity for liturgical ferment, coming as the result of a 1957 merger between the Congregational Christian Churches and the Evangelical and Reformed Church. The new denomination provided an opportunity for consolidating previous liturgical traditions, both Free Church and Reformed, and gave a fresh chance to start anew in liturgical construction. This had happened already in the Church of South India, where a new start presented the possibility of doing what none of the predecessor denominations had accomplished.

Time was also on the side of the United Church of Christ in that the final work came late enough after Vatican II for the latter liturgical products to be in contemporary English. But the disadvantages of moving too fast appeared in the quick scrapping of the 1969 "Lectionary" in favor of the Presbyterian version of the Roman Catholic three-year lectionary. This came about as a result of joint meetings with Presbyterians. Roman Catholics began using their new lectionary on November 30, 1969, and Presbyterians were the first to follow in 1970. Thus some liturgical projects are short-lived.

The United Church of Christ's Commission on Worship was established in 1960. To date, its most significant project has been the publication of two services of word and sacrament and an *ordo* for morning worship. These began with a single service in 1964, *The Lord's Day Service*, revised with the addition of a service in contemporary language in *Services of Word and Sacrament* of 1966, and subsequently issued in 1969 with both services now in contemporary language. In 1969 these services were published as part of a ring.book cover, *Services of the Church*, containing eight booklets. Thus appeared a novel form of service book—a collection comprising several booklets, all of the same format, with a different kind of service in each booklet. Leaflets can be added (or subtracted) as needs require. Small hymnal booklets, *A New Song* and *A New Song 2*, appeared in 1969 and 1971. This notebook of leaflets may well be the form that future service books will take, with updated inserts made available as needed.

The work was done by the UCC Commission on Worship, a group largely composed of pastors and seminary professors representing the antecedent denominations and reflecting rather strongly the Mercersburg liturgical tradition. The services of word and sacrament were largely prepared by a subcommittee of two Evangelical and Reformed pastors, a Congregational Christian pastor, and a Congregational Christian professor, and then discussed by the full Commission. The Commission operated for many years under the chairmanship of a seminary dean.

The idea of a liturgical establishment is rather antithetical to the lifelong habits of many Congregational pastors, and it would be interesting to know just how widely used is *Services of the Church*. A hard-bound hymnal organized around the UCC Statement of Faith was published in 1974, *Hymnal of the United Church of Christ*, including a number of new hymns. The United Church of Christ has bucked the trend toward denominational worship executives and thus has to operate without the advantages such individuals offer. Since 1973 some of those functions have been performed by persons in the office of Church Life and Leadership (289 Park Ave. South, New York, N.Y. 10010). Thus the UCC liturgical establishment consists of an official and constitutional, but volunteer, Commission.

If a liturgical establishment sounds like a self-contradiction for former Congregationalists, it seems all the stranger for the Christian Church (Disciples of Christ). Disciples have resisted much centralization in the past. Yet from 1968 to 1974 there was a staff position of director of worship program within the

Division of Homeland Ministries, and that board still carries on some of these functions (Box 1986, Indianapolis, IN 46206).

In 1966 a Commission on Worship was established for three years and another from 1970 to 1972. There seems to be little inclination to a permanent liturgical commission. During the six years a temporary Commission on Worship existed, it published *Worship in the Christian Church* (1969) and *In Spirit and with Honesty* (1973). Both of these publications were study guides to help local congregations in their decision-making processes. Neither included actual rites. The contributions of the Disciples' representatives to the COCU Commission on Worship have been outstanding for many years. Several seminary professors, well known as liturgical scholars, have been influential through individual publications, workshops, and the training of a new generation of ministers. Such influence can be pervasive in a denomination as loose-jointed as the Christian Church. It would be as possible to name the individual members of the Disciples' liturgical establishment as those of other denominations.

Three different hymnals have been produced by joint committees of the Disciples and the American Baptist Convention. *Christian Worship: A Hymnal* dates from 1941 and has been recently reprinted. A more recent production is *Hymnbook for Christian Worship,* published in 1970; while *Hymns and Songs of the Spirit* (1966) is intended for more informal use. There is a national Association of Disciples Musicians.

A significant ecumenical development in recent years has been the banding together of denominations in combined efforts at liturgical revision. One of the most notably successful of these joint enterprises has occurred among American Presbyterians. The 1946 *Book of Common Worship* never became common as a pew book, and the 1955 *Hymnbook* received a rather grudging acceptance by many who preferred its 1933 predecessor, *The Hymnal.* In the mid 1950s a Joint

Committee on Worship was formed by the Presbyterian Church in the United States, the United Presbyterian Church in the United States of America, and (later) the Cumberland Presbyterian Church. Sessions of the JCW were attended by an observer from the Reformed Church in America, a body that in 1965 finished preparing its own *Liturgy and Psalter* and published it in 1968. Members of the UCC Commission also participated for nearly a year.

The first significant accomplishment of the JCW was the production of a new *Directory for Worship* to replace the 1644 *Westminster Directory*, a worship book consisting entirely of rubrics. The new *Directory* was accepted by the United Presbyterian Church in 1961 as one of its constitutional documents. Next came a 1964 leaflet, *Service for the Lord's Day*, which included a two-year lectionary (later abandoned). JCW then produced a paperback volume, *The Book of Common Worship—Provisional Services*, in 1966. That was a chancy vintage, only two services being in contemporary language. Four years later, when *The Worshipbook—Services* appeared, traditional language had vanished altogether, although sensitivity had not yet risen enough to purge sexist terms. In 1972 the same service material was incorporated with service music and hymns in *The Worshipbook—Services and Hymns*. Thus, for the first time, American Presbyterians have a single pew volume containing all liturgical texts, service music, and hymns.

A significant development in the evolution of the *Worshipbook* was the use of a single editor to ensure consistency in the language. He ended his labors with a prayer "For Those Who Write Prayers" (p. 202). One person working thus consistently on questions of language was able to develop a perception of problems not so readily perceived by other denominations. He was helpful as a consultant in the production of the Methodist *Sacrament of the Lord's Supper*. Such expertise is a very real boon in current reform. Long usage has so accustomed us to unnecessary parallelisms, archaic words, and artificial cadences that we worship using such language hardly realizing its clash with the blunt, brash speech of our times. Presbyterians have advanced our search for "the straightforward use of words and language in current, contemporary use in the last third of the twentieth century."

Another step forward was the close and deliberately planned unity of the service material and the hymns. Hymn texts were rewritten to conform with the services, necessitating an "Index of Familiar Hymns with Unfamiliar First Lines." The hymns were arranged alphabetically. The coordination of hymnody and services has not been equaled by other denominations.

The work of the JCW was carried on by a large number of committee members and consultants, lay and clerical, representing the three denominations. Only one woman served on a committee. The chairmanship revolved around men from the several Presbyterian churches. At the 1974 General Assembly of the United Presbyterian Church the sexist nature of the *Worshipbook* language was challenged, but by then it was too expensive to revise the hardback volume published two years before. But it is refreshing to note that this and other issues concerning worship (adult baptism, communion of children) have been debated on the floor of the General Assembly.

In 1970 the Joint Office of Worship and Music was created with a full-time director, funded and utilized by the Presbyterian Church in the U.S. and the United Presbyterians. Beginning in late 1975, this became the Joint Office of Worship (Louisville Theological Seminary). Workshops, information as to resources, and the journal *Reformed Liturgy and Music* are energized by the director in cooperation with the Church Service Society and the Presbyterian Association of Musicians.

Lutherans have achieved a major ecumenical breakthrough through interdenominational liturgical cooperation. In the fall of 1966 the Inter-Lutheran Commission on Worship (ILCW) was organized by the Lutheran Church in America, the American Lutheran Church, the Lutheran Church-Missouri Synod, the Synod of Evangelical Lutheran Churches (later merged), and (later) the Evangelical Lutheran Church of Canada. Its purpose was to produce a service book for all American Lutherans, something never before accomplished. The LCA and the ALC had produced a joint service book and hymnal only eight years before, while the LC-MS's hymnal was a quarter of a century old. The LC-MS proceeded in 1969 to publish independently part of its previous work of revision as a soft-cover hymnal and service book, *Worship Supplement*. This salvage effort had some interesting aspects, especially a daily office in contemporary language, visual rubrics, and ninety-three hymns new to the LC-MS. Henceforth the churches worked together.

The Lutherans had a major asset going for them: a full-time staff in the area of worship. In this they preceded many other denominations and testified to Lutheran priorities. The LCA led the way with a worship executive who began work for the former United Lutheran Church of America on July 1, 1955; the ALC followed in 1963, and the LC-MS in 1967. Other assets were the annual Institute of Liturgical Studies and the Lutheran Society for Worship, Music, and the Arts. For these reasons, the ILCW utilizes only a small minority of seminary professors and seems to be more broadly based among pastors than the liturgical commissions of other churches.

The Lutheran efforts involved music right from the start, owing to this tradition's special strength in that area. For a time, the LCA and the ALC both had a second staff person with special responsibilities for church music. The LCA had for years a staff person in church architecture who worked to stress theological and liturgical suitability in building programs. The ILCW publications have placed a strong emphasis on hymnody and service music.

As in other cases of a new organization, the ILCW did what none of the constitutent members probably could have done. It began by looking ahead to creativity rather than backward to yet another revision. A fresh beginning was made by all four standing committees: hymn tunes, hymn texts, liturgical music, and liturgical texts. Each included representatives of all the churches involved. In turn, the liturgical texts committee was supplemented by a number of task forces. The first results of this work appeared in 1969 as a small paperback hymnal, *Contemporary Worship 1: Hymns,* including several folk songs.

The most significant of the *Contemporary Worship* series appeared in 1970 as *CW2: Services, The Holy Communion.* In a single leap forward, the chief branches of American Lutheranism proposed a service that was contemporary in language but classical in shape and content. An important commitment to the new age of pluralism occurred in the incorporation of four musical settings in modern classical, hymnic, chant, and folk music styles. *CW 2* was soon complemented by *CW 4: Hymns for Baptism and Holy Communion,* a 1972 collection of thirty hymns not available in current Lutheran hymnals. Even more significant was *CW 6: The Church Year, Calendar and Lectionary,* a 1973 release. It meant the giving up of certain distinctive Lutheran characteristics—for example, abandoning the Trinity season in favor of dating from Pentecost. A compromise was reached by including (in the back) the historic one-year lectionary retained by the Lutheran churches of Europe as well as the new Roman Catholic three-year lectionary, somewhat revised. Important innovations appear in the fresh calendar of saints, canonized and otherwise, and original and rewritten prayers of the day.

Work has moved into other areas as well. *CW 3: The Marriage Service* appeared in 1972 and is notable for the large amount of options it provides for adapting the wedding service. In 1972 appeared *CW 5: Services of the Word,* containing seasonal non-eucharistic services. More recent publications relate to baptism: *CW 7: Holy Baptism* (1974), and *CW 8: Affirmation of the Baptismal Covenant* (1975). *CW 8* represents a giant move forward by taking up the step the Episcopalians made in 1970 and then backed away from. Remarkably it coincides with the Methodist proposal which was developed at the same time without either church being aware of what the other was doing. The Lutheran proposal is all the more significant since Lutheran churches recently participated in a major study, *Confirmation and First Communion* (1968). They now propose possible elimination of even the word "confirmation," though, as with the Episcopalians, it might yet reappear.

Work is in progress on other services such as ordination, burial, and morning and evening prayer. Meanwhile, pressure has mounted for publication of a hard-cover service book and hymnal. Work on this, incorporating parts of the *CW* series, is well advanced and publication is anticipated in 1978 or 1979. The ILCW now supports a staff person (315 Park Ave. South, New York, N.Y. 10010) engaged primarily in work on the hard-cover book. Testing has followed the whole process. Some of the *CW* series include evaluation forms urging pastors to submit their reactions and reflections. As a result, revisions have already been prepared in some cases.

A major liturgical convocation was sponsored by Lutherans in Minneapolis in 1973 with strong ecumenical participation. Sessions helped interpret the proposed services, and some of the papers appeared in *Worship: Good News in Action.* This has been followed by a series of institutes on worship and music to help prepare for the new service book. Thus, the chains of communications have been strong and have increasingly bound Lutherans of various complexions together in closer unity.

The move for ecumenism has been strengthened even

further by the Commission on Worship of the Consultation on Church Union (228 Alexander St., Princeton, N.J. 08540). The Commission on Worship seems to have resulted from the desire of the COCU leadership to have a church ready—bell, book, and candle—whenever church union is achieved. In the interim, the Commission has set itself to serving the nine COCU churches.

The COCU Commission on Worship consists of two representatives from each of the nine COCU denominations. Meetings, held twice a year, have usually been attended by Lutheran, Roman Catholic, and American Baptist observers. Members include pastors, lay people, and a heavy representation of seminary professors. For many years the COCU Commission functioned as both a professional society for liturgical scholars and a clearinghouse for worship executives, functions now performed by more specialized groups. It thus provided a valuable forum for liturgical communication between the churches. The observers participated fully so that sessions often provided the clearest possible view of the liturgical establishment at work.

The COCU Commission's first major work was the production of a service to be used on ecumenical occasions and by individual churches. This was published in 1968 as *An Order of Worship*, and an edition with typographical changes appeared in 1970. The procedure used in this and subsequent publications was for the writer to produce a draft liturgy; bring it to a meeting where it was thoroughly discussed while he tried to ascertain the consensus on each point; taken back for fresh revision by the writer, further submissions, and final polishing before publication. Much had to be done by mail since travel could not come out of COCU's budget. The people doing this work were always heavily involved in their own denomination's revisions. COCU brought even greater pressure on their time but increased their contacts and ideas.

The initial success of *An Order of Worship* led to fresh

efforts. Next came *Holy Baptism,* published in 1973. It was a courageous undertaking because the Christian Church (Disciples of Christ) does not baptize infants, whereas the other eight churches do; nor do Disciples relish the use of creeds. Yet this effort, for which the writer was a Disciple, produced a variable service designed to be adapted for the baptism of both adults and children. Meanwhile COCU had produced "The Ordinal," though not by the liturgists. Heavy criticism from them led to considerable modification before publication in *A Plan of Union* in 1970.

The Commission's third product, *A Lectionary,* appeared in 1974. This took the lectionaries recently produced (Roman Catholic, Episcopal, Lutheran, and Presbyterian) and attempted, insofar as possible, to produce a consensus lectionary. Perhaps even more significant was the agreement on a COCU calendar, printed in *A Lectionary.* The lectionary and calendar have been widely used, especially by United Methodists, who have offered these as alternatives to those in the *Book of Worship.* COCU has work underway on a common psalter project. This should be a significant boon to many churches, such as the Presbyterians, who omitted this difficult but important work. Also under preparation is a second-generation and more flexible order of worship.

COCU serves a large segment of American Christianity, but the International Consultation on English Texts reaches a much larger constituency, namely the majority of English-speaking Christians around the world. Several agencies feed into the ICET. The Roman Catholic ICEL has already been mentioned. Related to COCU, but broader, was the Consultation on Common Texts, which tried to reach agreement among American Christians on basic liturgical texts such as the Lord's Prayer. The CCT Lord's Prayer appeared in COCU's *Order of Worship.*

The ICET was established in 1969 as an international and ecumenical body to translate and revise the basic liturgical texts that most churches use regularly or occasionally. COCU and three American churches are represented on the ICET, as well as churches in Ireland, Scotland, Wales, England, and Australia. It is jointly chaired by two Englishmen, an Anglican and a Roman Catholic. The result of the ICET's labors is *Prayers We Have in Common,* originally published in 1970. Two types of texts were then included: those on which agreement had been reached and others in process. An enlarged and revised edition appeared in 1971 in which this distinction had disappeared. And a second revised edition came out in 1975, the result of three years of test use. Many of the texts have been adopted by various denominations of the English-speaking world. Particular problems arose with the sixth petition of the Lord's Prayer and the *Filioque* clause in the Nicene Creed. But the texts of the Lord's Prayer, Apostles' Creed, Nicene Creed, Kyrie, Gloria in Excelsis, Sursum Corda, Sanctus and Benedictus, Agnus Dei, Gloria Patri, and canticles have been widely used throughout the English-speaking world. ICET texts have set a kind of international standard for liturgical prose, though they have been adopted on a rather inconsistent basis. Apparently the Lord's Prayer remains the chief object of holdout in favor of traditional language. The ICET has managed to focus more theological and literary scholarship on a problem all the churches share than any of them could have brought together in isolation.

I have described the work of the nine official agencies constituting the liturgical establishment. None of these operates in isolation from the others. There is also an unofficial liturgical establishment of various publications, organizations, and centers. None of these is authorized or funded directly by the denominations that support the establishment. Yet the members and work of these bodies mesh so completely with the official agencies that it would be misleading to fail to mention the unofficial groups. I will limit myself to a brief catalog of them.

Preeminent is the publication *Worship*, a bimonthly inaugurated a half century ago, in 1926, and still published by the Benedictine monks of St. John's Abbey (Collegeville, Minn. 56321). For decades it virtually was the liturgical movement in American Roman Catholicism and now is a strong ecumenical force for liturgical renewal. *Studia Liturgica* is a scholarly quarterly published in the Netherlands (P.O.B. 25088, Rotterdam) though written in English. It represents the devoted work of one man who has continued its publication through financial thick and thin (mostly thin) since 1962. A most useful practical publication is *Liturgy*, a monthly published for the last twenty years by the Liturgical Conference (1330 Massachusetts Ave. N.W., Washington D.C. 20005). This group originated in 1940 as a Roman Catholic pressure group but has become thoroughly ecumenical. It maintains a staff in Washington D.C. and has put out a number of publications and held some very important national liturgical weeks. A useful service is performed by the Celebration Centre of the United Church of Canada (85 St. Clair Ave. E., Toronto M4T 1M8) which publishes quarterly an annotated catalogue of resources of books, music, and records, *Getting It All Together*.

Liturgical organizations exist within several denominations: Associated Parishes (Episcopal) (Box 5562, Washington, D.C. 20016); United Methodist Society for Worship (P.O. Box 840, Nashville, TN 37202); the Church Service Society (Presbyterian; Louisville Theological Seminary, Louisville, KY 40205); and the Lutheran Society for Worship Music and the Arts (Valparaiso University, Valparaiso, IN 46383). The most recent organization is the North American Academy of Liturgy (Box 81, Notre Dame, IN 46556), established in 1975 as the professional society of liturgical scholars. Another scholarly organization is Societas Liturgica, a group with European conventions, occasional papers, and worldwide membership (American treasurer: President, New Brunswick Theological Seminary, New Brunswick, N.J. 08901). The Association of Worship Executives (AWE) is a liturgical clearinghouse for denominational executives (P.O Box 840, Nashville, TN 37202).

There are also liturgical centers. The Florida-based World Center for Liturgical Studies, now closed, was for years largely the consecrated labor of an individual. It specialized in week-long conferences. The Center for Contemporary Celebration (Box 3024 West Lafayette, IN 47906) focuses heavily on music while not neglecting the other arts. It has produced several publications and conducts workshops on location. The Center for Worship Reformation (1219 Third St. N.W., Salem, OR 97304) has held a number of workshops and sends out a monthly publication, *Worship Pac*. The Murphy Center for Liturgical Research (Box 81, Notre Dame, IN 46556) has held a number of significant conferences and issues a newsheet, *Hucusque*. The Institute of Liturgical Studies (Valparaiso University, Valparaiso, IN 46383) has conducted annual conventions since 1949. There are other publications, organizations, and centers not listed here, but these would seem to be representative. They often can operate with a freedom that an official agency may not quite achieve without offending portions of its constituency. Thus these bodies provide a valuable service in pioneering and testing new possibilities.

II

I now raise our key question: Just how well has this liturgical establishment served the churches? It must be remembered that it operated in a period without precedent in the history of the church. No one anticipated the ferment of 1966–75, and our hindsight wisdom ought to be tempered with recognition of just how unexpected the events of the recent past have been for us all.

It is inherently unlikely that committees will be very radical or even very creative. Most of them are carefully selected so as to represent a large constituency, thus canceling out extremes. A flight to the center usually ensues. Despite this, much of the liturgical establishment has been well ahead of its constituency throughout this period. Thus the establishment has been on the cutting edge of the church, though not as finely honed as some individuals. But it is unrealistic to compare the work of committees with that of creative individuals. As suggested in chapter 5, both have their places, but they are two distinct and separate places that complement each other. Creative individuals can always go further and faster.

Having said this, I should state that committees have taken the lead in certain instances, particularly with regard to Christian initiation. And I would argue that it has been largely the work of committees that has led us to a commonly acceptable contemporary liturgical language. Like music and architecture, language should not call excessive attention to itself in worship but should be a servant. ("As he grows greater, I must grow less"—John 3:30.) Individuals have made highly personal contributions in this area, but a language that is not distinctive or distinguished may be preferable. Worship committees have also been in the forefront in working for and reaping the benefits of church unity.

A common problem in all liturgical committee work is the invariable tendency for each member to say: "Well this is already far too long, but certainly it should include such and such." Conciseness is not a trait of committees. Everyone gets his or her oar in, and though the result may be more representative, it is rarely succinct. Individuals usually avoid this pitfall but may have less balanced results in their texts.

Another factor must appear in our evaluation. Just how much support have the churches given their liturgical establishment? Excepting the Roman Catholic Church, the establishment has had to depend largely on understaffed, underfunded, volunteer work. Surprisingly, this has not been a high priority area for most American churches. Only two Protestant denominations had a full-time worship executive for the duration of this entire decade. All too often, committees have simply been unable to meet for lack of funds. Just how much work can be accomplished when a committee meets only twice a year? Even more neglected has been widespread testing and evaluation in many cases. Some denominations operate without a worship executive, though they would not think of working without executives in fields such as Christian education. Serious questions ought to be raised about the priorities of some churches.

Most of the work done has been volunteer work by very busy pastors, teachers, and lay people. This raises the question: Why not do more of the work together? We have seen in this chapter frequent repetition of labors; every church has to produce a funeral service. The results of joint efforts would probably be superior to denominational ones. As shown in chapter 3, the various traditions are tending to mingle today, and such cross-fertilization usually produces better fruit. In a time of financial stringency, more cooperative efforts are desirable.

We must also question how representative the establishment has been. Increasingly an effort has been made to include blacks, hispanics, women, and youth on worship commissions. But all too often these people have remained silent during discussions or not appeared for meetings. They are often intimidated by the "experts," and so the minority input often remains minimal even when representatives are physically present. I have a strong suspicion that the print-media focus of worship commissions is distant from the needs of some minorities. Had women members been more outspoken, we might have been spared the redoing of some work that now appears dated.

As in courtship, so in liturgical revision, timing is all-important. We have seen several stages emerge already—the traditional language, the breakthrough to contemporary language, and now the realization of just how sexist much of that was. We moved to a new (and very old) shape for the eucharist and are just on the verge of the biggest change in initiation since the Reformation. If our consciousness is raised today so that sexist language becomes intolerable, what will be next? In other words, nothing is likely to stay nailed down for very long. Work becomes dated very fast because the rate of change has accelerated so much. This means a whole new dimension for our work—openness to change. When Methodists approved new service books in 1964, they thought they were through for another generation. They had just begun! Change had become a basic condition of liturgical work.

This new condition raises a great many questions about the advisability of publishing hard-cover service books. These can hardly be managed financially more often than once every twenty years without congregations feeling they have not yet amortized the previous edition. Thus it seems likely that more service books—especially the second- and third-generation services of the 1970s—will be published in forms that suggest impermanence and transience. This in turn will facilitate further revision. Thus change becomes permanent itself and sets up conditions for further change. Unfortunately such transient publications are often rushed into production with little concern for quality liturgical graphics, even though we increasingly realize that the appearance of a page may say as much to the worshiper as its contents. Good design is too important to be sacrificed for production speed. The liturgical committees that produce these books will probably become standing liturgical committees whose work is never done, rather than temporary *ad hoc* groups.

We are faced with the problem of those outside the establishment. In a sense, they can always buy into it. But how can the establishment learn from their experiences? We have not resolved this very well. There seems to be a widening communication gap between the churches served directly by the liturgical establishment and those outside its reach.

On the whole, though, we must say that the liturgical establishment has served the churches very well in a most difficult time. There has been more originality and creativity than we might have had reason to expect. Hopefully we have learned from our mistakes and they have not been disastrous. Best of all, we have learned to live with change without losing our historical roots and have, in many cases, affirmed our roots more securely. The liturgical establishment has helped to keep our worship current, yet rooted in the traditions of the whole church. For this we must give thanks.

VII

After Experimentation (1975)

The decade 1966–1975 produced irrevocable changes in Roman Catholic and Protestant worship. The changes were both more rapid and more radical than any Christianity has experienced in the last four hundred years. Much of the heady glow of that period is now behind us, and it is increasingly apparent that we have already turned another corner in worship. In 1970 I was confident that the electronic media had brought about many of the changes we were then experiencing in worship and that the media themselves would be widely used in worship in the future. It is indicative that those electronic media are hardly mentioned in this book.

For many people the late 1960s and early 1970s will be remembered as the period in which the phrase "experimental worship" became common. I am much more prone today to attribute the primary roots of experimental worship to an increased sensitivity to the pluralistic aspects of American culture than to the electronic media, though the media certainly helped raise our consciousness of pluralism. Today we are experiencing quite other factors in our thought and practice of worship.

I would contend that the period of experimentation has already been absorbed by many of us as a part of our history just as had previous periods of change in worship. For many congregations, experimentation has become a standard and permanent part of their worship. When so routinized as to become a normal expectation, "experimentation" hardly seems to be an appropriate term any longer. The rate of change has accelerated. Previous periods of transition in worship usually took much longer to run their courses.

Certainly experimentation brought its disappointments and disillusions. Obviously it did not change everything as some dreamed it might. All the other plugging along for renewal had to continue too. Experimentation meant more work for everyone, a lot more for the pastor. We soon found our ideas ran dry. And many of us soon discovered how ill equipped we were to be very creative about worship. One constantly heard pastors say: "I'd like to try some things, but my people would never allow it." Freely translated that meant: "I'm threatened because I don't have any sure-fire ideas, and I might end up looking foolish." Things were not helped either by some pastors who inflicted experimentation on congregations without taking the people into their confidence. Such situations were almost sure to be counterproductive. These failures in communication gave others excuses not to trouble Israel by even attempting experimentation.

I am very much aware that there are plenty of pastors and congregations that have escaped any contact with experimentation. There are plenty of churches whose worship life is still the same today as before experimentation.

But many of us have increasingly realized that we have now entered a stage after experimentation. We cannot go back to understanding and practicing worship as we once did. Experimentation has affected us in ways that are irrevocable. The period of experimentation has become lodged as a permanent part of us. I shall try to help crystallize the lasting residue of this period so we can examine it. I propose to sort out these permanent results as five distinct aspects.

I

During the last few years, we have been forced to become more *inclusive* in our thinking about the people who worship. It has taken a lot of experience, both in the church and outside, to make us realize just how exclusive our approach to people had been. We provided what we thought was good for people, and they liked it or they left. Many left. This made us recognize how narrow and limited the options that we offered in worship were. Like Henry Ford with his Model T, we had been providing in worship a choice of one color (black). Yet daily we became more conscious of how richly varied and pluralistic American society was as the melting-pot mentality gave way to a whole spectrum of ethnic prides. Belatedly we began to fashion our worship around the reality of a variety of people living together in a pluralistic culture.

Increasingly we came to realize in how many subtle ways our worship excluded some and insulted others. Our very respectability affronted many for whom security and comfort were no longer prime goals in life. We finally realized how casually we overlooked children and women. One had to be an adult to worship God in a service that used big words and no large muscles. Some women might be delighted to sing "God Send Us Men," but that was not why it was placed in denominational hymnals along with a host of other hymns that implied that the church was only masculine. We had to unlearn much and to learn new ways of showing we respected and cared for different types of people.

The most obvious outcome of this recognition of pluralism in society and the consequent move to inclusivism in worship has been the emergence all over this country of three different models for services. The first of these models I call "eclectic." It is the type of service which is carefully planned to reflect a cross section of the congregation. In the prayers appear the anxieties of both liberals and conservatives, the music varies from gospel song to Bach to folk song or further, and the language ranges from Cranmer to Malcolm Boyd. Purists decry this type of polyglot service, but it has advantages. It certainly demands that the pastor and worship committee know the people to whom they are ministering.

The second pattern is the occasional service in which on certain Sundays the whole service is in a style congenial to a particular segment of the congregation. This may mean a youth Sunday once a month. This has some advantage to the purist and also is easier to plan and staff. But it is also easier to disregard if one feels one is not in the group primarily involved—unless, of course, the style of each service is not announced in advance. These first two patterns are possible in churches of any size.

A third pattern has developed in many large congregations. This is the multiple-service route. A number of different styles and occasions of worship are offered. Frequently they occur in different spaces and at different hours. One goes where one feels most natural. Such a system is rather difficult to staff and populate except in large congregations, but it has received favorable responses in a number of these. In effect, it means the development of several communities within a large congregation.

Far less obvious, but a subtle result of the new inclusivism, has been a more free and spontaneous attitude to worship in general. Most congregations still have a grim determination to get from the top left corner of the bulletin to the bottom right by high noon. But they might not be as upset now as they once would have been if they got derailed along the way or got out ten minutes early or late.

Another shift has come in the role of the pastor as director of Christian worship. The pastor tends to share his or her responsibilities and relies on more and more other people. Sometimes the pastor has become more a coordinator or even a producer than a one-person show. This became almost inevitable when we began to think and act about worship in an inclusive manner.

II

The role of the pastor and others responsible for worship planning and leadership has changed in another fashion. We have come to recognize the importance of *imagination* in planning worship. Much of the challenge and excitement in worship leadership in recent years has come because of this new demand for imagination. In order to make worship less exclusive, we were compelled to try many things we had never done before. After the first few plunges, we found the water was not bad at all and some soon became pretty expert swimmers.

A major hurdle was passed once we started experimenting and came to realize the tyranny of fixed assumptions. Let me illustrate: It was found on one major campus in Illinois that the most convenient time for university students to attend worship was midnight Saturday night on the way home from dates. When would that hour ever have occurred to the average congregation? We found that we had been locked in by a whole array of other fixed assumptions about worship, all of them as arbitrary as the eleven o'clock Sunday time. It took imagination to discover and to create fresh alternatives. If we moved out of the usual church building, we found all kinds of possibilities were open to us in the fellowship hall, where nothing was nailed down. Assumptions about clothing, bulletins, seating, and on and on were challenged. Then we had to create something new and better to take their place.

It became apparent to many that Christian worship cried out for variety. Yet Sunday after Sunday the average congregation was greeted by a building always the same for all occasions, and most of the services in it had little more variety. For many, the realization that you could change the context of the building and, in effect, have a new building every Sunday, led to other means of adding variety to worship. Somewhere along the way, the traditional Christian year was rediscovered as what it had always been—the chief asset we have for stimulating imagination and variety in worship. The Christian year became a convenient pegboard on which to hang our ideas and prodded us to fill in all those vacant pegholes.

Once our creative instincts were turned loose, we began to

recognize the tremendous variety of possibilities in planning worship. No longer was worship seen as something one just took out of the book. Rather it demanded a visual imagination, creative use of space, a willingness to explore a variety of art forms, sensitive use of the whole body, and the ability to experiment with a whole new range of sounds and sights.

The catch was that more and more this demanded a trained imagination. Most ministers who began experimenting soon found a great gulf between a well-meaning imagination and a trained imagination. An architect can see possibilities in lighting and space that others cannot imagine simply because they have not been trained to do so. We soon realized that one person's imagination is not enough. It became more and more necessary to rely upon conferences and publications and especially on trained people in our own community.

Increasingly this meant, as I have indicated, that the minister found himself or herself coordinating the creative efforts of a number of people. Instead of simply pecking out on the typewriter, in the privacy of the study, the weekly bulletin, prayers, and sermon, the minister spent more and more time on the telephone making sure each one had prepared his or her contribution for the service. A pastor relying only on his or her own imagination became just as out of place as the preacher who never checks a commentary to benefit from other people's interpretations of scripture. We learned the lesson of interdependence in worship. Worship leadership became, in effect, a political activity in which the pastor organized available resources for the mutual benefit of the whole worshiping community.

III

A third consequence of the past decade has been our developing an approach to worship as a more fully *humanizing* experience involving our whole being. It is an irony that one as intensely intellectual as Calvin grasped the importance of sign-acts as God's way of accommodating himself to our capacity to understand him, yet Calvin's descendants have treated sign-acts so lightly. In our own time, Edward Schillebeeckx seems to echo Calvin on humans' need for signs. Perhaps at last we are ready to accept our need for the signs God provides for giving himself to us.

We have become more convinced that worship is far more than words as we grew more conscious of our obsession with saying the right things in worship and our compulsion to get through the bulletin. Human expression is wider and broader than words alone, though we cannot dispense with words either. Our culture has seen a rediscovery of the body and senses as part of being fully human. Worship is not a disincarnate affair; our very bodies are signs of love. The very act of assembling to discern the Lord's body may be more important than anything said in Christian worship. Philosophers and others have schooled us in how deeply all the senses are involved in perception. Theologically it may make little difference whether a baby is baptized with a teaspoonful or a tubfull. (Indeed, I have seen many baptisms where one wonders whether it might have been a dry run, at least at the head end.) But the sign value of the actual act of washing and cleansing with life-giving water makes *how* baptism is done a matter of prime importance for the way worshipers perceive the sacrament. We have become sensitive to the sign value of actions and things.

Closely related is a new concern with all the arts. It used to be possible, sometimes tempting, to go through worship with our eyes shut. Now our eyes have been opened. Most of us went through a banner stage, and many of us preachers have to confess that we remember more banners we have seen than sermons we have heard. Banners were important, for they taught us how to see. That was a major step but not the last one. We learned a whole gamut of new sounds, a new spectrum of sights. Architecture and music were joined by graphics, photography, mime, dance, ceramics, textiles, and other art forms as indispensable church arts. In all this, we discovered anew how important architecture is in setting the agenda for the other arts. We also found how many people with a variety of artistic abilities there are in every community and how delighted they often are to contribute their talents to worship. The arts played an important part in humanizing worship by scaling things to our dimensions and capacities.

Preaching, too, underwent a general loosening up, a move away from the authoritarian monologue to the sharing of authority. It meant at times that the preacher both literally and figuratively had to come down to the level of the congregation and stop speaking over its head. Part of the vitality of preaching has been shown in its ability to adapt to changing human scenes. Recent efforts to get the sermon out of the pulpit and into the pew show that preaching is alive and well.

Many people have assumed that the central aspect of experimentation in worship was the change in words. It is true that the spoken language has changed drastically and irrevocably. But to assume that the change has been primarily a change in style rather than in content is to miss the point altogether. Cranmer wrote only a hundred fifty years after Chaucer's death and more than four hundred years from our time. It was relatively simple to exchange Cranmer's language for one of our own times. But Cranmer taught us not just the words; he taught us how to pray. Take away the words, and we had to find a new way to pray too. No longer can we go home to a safe way of praying in nicely balanced cadences that presume a well-balanced universe. We ended up having to pray as people of our times, and it was not easy. Fortunately there were people like Huub Oosterhuis who helped us see how deeply imbedded prayer was in all varieties of human experience. How we pray had to change just as surely as the words we used. We can no longer go home to Cranmer's world, and so prayer has become a more radical lifting up of our hearts than we ever expected.

IV

In the past decade, worship, both Protestant and Catholic, has become much more *ecumenical*. Basically this happened without anyone's organizing a committee or forming an organization. When you needed something you simply borrowed the best that was available, and denominational labels meant little. In 1965 it was still possible to distinguish seven distinct Protestant traditions of worship. Today, except for the Quakers, the chief differences often appear to be within traditions, not between them. When Pentecostal and Anglican traditions mingle, when Free Churchmen and Roman Catholics borrow from each other, it is obvious that we have entered a new ball game.

One hears of a Methodist bishop celebrating the Roman mass and of the Catholic Bishops' Committee on the Liturgy *Newsletter* publishing the 1972 United Methodist communion service. Imagine that in 1960! Take away the title pages of the eucharistic rites of the 1970s, and one would be hard put to tell which denomination composed which. Surely, the new Roman Catholic lectionary is Catholicism's greatest gift to Protestant preaching, just as Protestant biblical scholarship has given so much impetus to Catholic preaching. Borrowing became the surest and best form of grass-roots ecumenism. Anyone who has discovered riches this way is not apt ever again to be content with the wealth of a single tradition.

Less spectacular, but even more significant, has been a renewed interest in the sacraments among Protestants. Here, too, there has been sharing in both forms and in theology. Many found that the sacraments suggested far more possibilities for experimentation than did non-sacramental worship. The centrality of the mass in Roman Catholic worship stimulated many Protestants to desire more frequent eucharistic celebrations. More recently, the center of interest has passed fundamental restructuring of the whole process of Christian initiation.

It may seem paradoxical, but during the last decade the newest thing has often been a recovery of old forms of worship from our earliest history. In a post-Constantinian era, pre-Constantinian worship was bound to have its appeal. Hippolytus, who did everything he could to halt experimentation in the third century, has provoked plenty of it in the twentieth. All renewal movements tend to look back in history, and it's not strange that we often meet other traditions also taking a new look at the worship of the early and undivided church. We have become aware of just how recent much which we took to be normative was. Our history is older by far than the prejudices of the oldest member of the congregation.

We rediscovered how infinitely variable and flexible the hard core of Christian worship has been without losing its essential consistency. Basically what has happened in the last ten years is that we have recovered the perennial tradition and expressed it in terms of our times. History became for us a liberating discipline that encouraged and stimulated further experimentation.

V

In recent years worship has displayed a greater sense of *social responsibility*. Much of the ferment in worship has been deeply connected with the struggle for social justice. This relationship may be easy to observe; it is difficult to state precisely the reasons for it.

One possibility is that those most interested in worship reform were also the people most active in working for social reforms. This is relatively easy to document. Most of the leading social activists in the Roman Catholic Church seemed to belong to the Liturgical Conference. Speakers invited to its national liturgical weeks often included such well-known "liturgists" as Saul Alinsky, Cèsar Chavez, and the Black Panthers. Most of us know the congregations in our own areas that are most deeply concerned with liturgical renewal. Almost always the same congregations are in the forefront of working for social change. But what is the relationship? Is it just that people and congregations that are turned on seem to be lively in all dimensions of their life together? And do the other people and congregations, content with business as usual, just miss everything? No, it must lie deeper than that.

Those in the forefront of liturgical change have not been the sacristy-rat type, worrying about the cut of the chasuble, but rather the activists, planning a service of repentance for Vietnam. These people have been motivated by a sense of honesty that despised liturgical false fronts as much as social shams. Their sense of integrity had to cut both ways. "Tell it like it is" was a slogan a few years back, and it applied to sacraments and politics alike. In other words, the sense of integrity those persons and congregations possessed made it impossible for them to work for social change without also stimulating liturgical change, nor could they work for worship renewal without engaging in the struggle for justice.

There are a variety of other factors too. New seriousness about the sacraments confronted us with how human, worldly, and materialistic the Christian God is. I remember first being propelled into politics by the realization that "This is my body" means "This is my precinct." And baptism jumped out at us as the ultimate condemnation of racism and sexism. Somehow we had forgotten that Paul had told us the same thing (Gal. 3:27-28). The Christian sacraments became a strong incentive to fight for justice.

In the same way, the changes in the language and content of

prayer made action for social change inevitable too. The new language of prayer in its avoidance of contrived beauty and artificial euphony made it easier to see God's hands dirty in this world. You could not express concern about drinking water in the *barrios* or the exploitation of prostitutes while using Cranmerian English, but then such concerns might have never occurred to you while praying with a Cranmerian mentality. A new directness and specificity in prayer pointed to a greater worldliness. Maybe we learned, at last, to pray as if the world was indeed our parish. The widespread adoption of spontaneous prayer of intercession coming from the congregation undoubtedly was a factor in this down-to-earthiness. Such prayer tended to displace the long or pastoral prayer which was all too often known for its vague and lofty generalizations. The real change was not in the language of prayer but in how we prayed. A direct, concrete, and specific concern with prayer has gone hand in hand with efforts for social change.

Likewise, the removal of many of the encrustations of worship made many realize how worship and the struggle for justice were both cut from the same cloth—the service of God. When the shreds of respectability were ripped away, worship was seen to be not just a cozy way of affirming our comfort and security but a means of rejoicing and suffering with all humanity.

The late 1960s and early 1970s taught us that worship and social concern went hand in hand. Sacraments and politics were closer than we had ever expected.

We were changed in important ways as we went through a decade of experimentation in worship. We shall never be quite the same again. Some of the things that happened to us seem irrevocable, especially the lessons that worship must be inclusive, imaginative, humanizing, ecumenical, and socially responsible. These lessons, distilled out of the turmoil of the period, will shape whatever comes next as God's people continue to rejoice in their Creator.

VIII
The Church
Architecture of Change

When we are gone, our buildings remain; when a period is past, its architecture endures. Buildings tell us what was important for people, whether it was ostentation, sentimentality, comfort, or discipline. The church architecture of the last few years has already frozen our experiences into visual history. We can see ourselves reflected in these structures as they crystallize our recent past. What do the church buildings of the last decade say of us and to us?

No doubt they say many things. But one thing seems to stand out: We learned that the forms of worship were subject to change, and this changed all our thinking about church architecture. For the first time in history, we had to build not for *a* particular change but for change itself as a permanent reality. Our church architecture had not only to accept the possibility of change but to make it feasible.

One of the best ways to realize what such a revolution in church architecture means is to stop for a moment in the 1970s to see where we have come from in the past decade. In analyzing so short a period as ten years, we become aware of how different the realities of the present are from those of the recent past. Those concepts that seem so true and obvious today were not so a decade ago. The changes in church architecture, from a confident architecture of permanence to a humbler architecture of change, tell us much about what happened to ourselves.

I must confess that I write these pages with a deep sense of personal involvement. My book *Protestant Worship and Church Architecture* (1964) was used, for better or for worse, by a couple of thousand building committees in the 1960s. Now it is out of print, and I have no further stake in it. But it does help me compare those things which seemed to me so true and obvious when it was written in 1963 with what I can observe today. The book was written, of course, before the *Constitution on the Sacred Liturgy* had been promulgated or anyone had heard the word "experimentation" applied to worship. What has happened architecturally since then is a good outward and visible sign of how our worship has changed.

I shall try to describe the differences, then, between the pace-setting church buildings of the mid-sixties and those of the mid-seventies. In either case, we are dealing with the minority of the churches actually built; many, if not most, new churches, then as now, reflect a worship-as-usual attitude. People are still keeping the faith by mimicking the buildings built in New England from 1790 to 1830, as if to keep a golden age alive. And just as one assumes that Gothic at long last has been priced out of the market, one finds oil-rich communities in Texas or Oklahoma who had not heard. The pace-setting buildings, I would take it, are those most widely publicized in the architectural journals, in *Faith and Form,* and those granted awards at such meetings as the Guild for Religious Architecture conventions.

I think we have since 1965 gone through a period of revulsion against church architecture in which many of us wondered whether a church concerned about mission had any reason to build. It must be said to the credit of many of the finest church architects that they were raising the question, Who needs us? just as vigorously as the clergy were debating the morality of building. We are past that phase, I think, and better off because it occurred. For it made us see that a building can be a tool in mission and that that is its only purpose. And it made us realize just what a powerful tool architecture can be for good or evil. Several of the pioneering congregations that began by denying the usual pattern of building ended up by building too. As we got more and more into experimentation, we realized how much the building sets the agenda and that good buildings could work with us just as much as bad ones could thwart us. Architecture, we learned, opens possibilities for us or takes them away. So we came out of this stage with a much healthier respect for architecture as a tool in mission.

I should like to analyze five basic differences between the churches we were building in the 1960s from those we are building today. Perhaps this will help give us some guidance for the next few years.

I

One of the principal factors affecting church building in recent years has been neither theological nor aesthetic. It has been simply a matter of *economics*. The 1960s saw the last flush of a booming era of church building. For the first of that period, over a billion dollars per year was being spent in this country for church building. As the sixties progressed, that sum was reduced but even more significant was that the number of projects was diminishing as inflation eroded the amount of building the total represented. The increasing cost of money was another factor in postponing and diminishing building projects. Now that money has become even tighter and building costs even higher, the amount of new building of any type has dropped still further.

This may be more of a blessing than we had realized. One of the regrettable facts about churches built in the fifties and sixties was that they were so fine and expensive. As our needs in worship changed, we found that we had built terribly expensive buildings which fought any adaptation. How hard it is to change something built out of cut stone! Indeed, what a sense of permanence and unchanging liturgical life such an anachronistic building material suggests!

I am sure that many others have felt the same urge I sometimes have when worshiping in these expensive, cold, formal buildings. I want to get a can of spray paint and spray some bright red crosses and words of hope on elegant

Georgian columns or over-intricate Gothic arches. Any sign of life would help. Some of these elegant, expensive churches make me crave the store-front political office where anything relevant or impish gets taped up on the peeling plaster walls. How much more life such places have!

Frankly, a lot of those buildings were so expensive that we are forever intimidated by them. The pastor worked hard to raise the money, the donors are still around, and the word is "hands off." Had we been poorer, had our hopes been more modest, we might be better served by these buildings today.

Economic circumstances have changed that and quite possibly to our advantage. God does work in mysterious ways! Many of the best churches built since World War II were those built in Europe where money was tight. There there was no extra money for gilding the lily. Many of the new European churches are honest, direct, and straightforward. As a result, they often have an aesthetic quality that many of ours miss. One American architect has a slide show of the church of a congregation that got more and more money and kept adding things to the interior of their building. He ends by showing the original slide and, without a word, the point is clear: they did not know when to stop. Economics are teaching us to know when to stop. We are learning the discipline of poverty.

This means that in recent years we have had to concentrate on essentials. What is absolutely basic for our use? And what is not? We are forced to ask these questions again and again and to concentrate on *utility*, building only what we absolutely must have and use. The rest we can do without; we may be better off without it. Had the same economic factors been operative in the early sixties as today, we might be better served by what we built then than we now are.

II

A second major change is closely related to the first; a change in *construction methods* has been forced upon us largely because of economic factors. Today we would not think (though some might dream) of building a traditional timber-framed barn when we can build a post barn with metal sheathing so much cheaper. The same thing applies to churches. When you have to look again and again at the building costs per square foot, you begin to accept some realities you never before contemplated. This, too, may be a blessing.

One of the best churches I have seen recently was built with the same tilt-slab construction as the supermarket next door and at a remarkably low cost. Other new churches are being built with construction methods we usually associate with warehouses—cement block walls, flat roofs, and exposed steel trusses. Supermarkets and warehouses, buildings calculated to return the maximum yield for the minimum expense—these are going to be our models from here on in. And why not? The church should be every bit as concerned about making the most of available resources as any business firm is. The irony is that these building methods can produce churches whose utility is just as great or greater than elegant cut-stone structures. In the hands of a competent architect, I would argue, they can be buildings of equal beauty. The challenge of limited resources may enhance the beauty. At least you know when to stop, if you ever get started!

Construction methods that we have associated solely with secular building types are going to be used more and more for churches. Theologically it makes sense, too. As Dean Joseph Mathews says, "He's a sneaky God." We find the holy in the midst of the ordinary; sacred and secular are kith and kin.

Many of the best new churches have shown a different sense of scale. We are more inclined now to look at a church as a social part of the townscape which fits in with its neighbors rather than as a monument which dominates them. Too long our ideal was the New England village church that provided a landmark for the surrounding countryside. We simply transplanted these churches to the city. I know of one ultra-elegant Georgian church in a Southern city that has the words "Night Cometh" on the clockface of its tower. When high-rise bachelor apartments surrounded it, those quaint words took on new and less theological meaning.

Recently we have developed a sense of church buildings built on a domestic scale. One of the best new churches in the Minneapolis area was deliberately scaled to the dimensions of the surrounding single-family residences. An irony of much historic preservation has been our tendency to preserve the great house but to ignore the shacks of slaves (in this country) or serfs (in Russia) who made the great house possible. Perhaps today we have finally realized that the church belongs in the village, gathered about the gates of the great house, and not on the broad lawns of the estate itself. A servant people does not need mansions. Churches are going to complement their neighborhoods now rather than dominate them.

Writing as I am in an impoverished part of Vermont, where virtually all new building permits are issued for pre-fabs and mobile homes, I believe this may well mean more and more use of standardized building components in churches too. But then we are only talking about extent. Ever since nails began to be made in factories instead of locally by hand, we have had standardization to a certain degree. In my farmhouse no two nails are the same, for they were made by hand before 1800. But in the village there are several houses that came intact out of the same factory. The larger the standardized component becomes, the greater the challenge to use it creatively.

Using a domestic scale as our point of reference is nothing new. One need not go back as far as the early church for point of contact. Dissenters' chapels in eighteenth-century England were deliberately built on domestic models to avoid destruction by establishment mobs. And many of the establishment's own churches in eighteenth-century Virginia, built at remote country crossroads where towers would have no use, are clearly domestic in appearance. The same was true of many meetinghouses erected in New England until about 1790. Perhaps most consistent were the Quaker meetinghouses which, except for the two doors (for men and women separately), almost always resembled dwelling houses.

As we move from a monumental scale to a domestic one, we discover some advantages we had missed before. As we look for "that full, conscious, and active participation in liturgical celebrations" which the fathers of Vatican II tell us is "the right and duty" of Christian people "by reason of their baptism," we realize the advantages of *intimacy* in liturgical space. Much of what seems desirable to us in worship today can be enhanced by a smaller edifice and defeated by a vast monument. I once heard Pope Paul VI preach against triumphalism in the church, but St. Peter's Basilica shouted him down.

The most endearing quality about so many small country churches is how intimately they involve the whole congregation present in the liturgical action. There are no dead spaces, no columns to hide behind; everyone is right out on the fifty-yard line. I think we shall see much more church building that is constructed on a more domestic scale where everyone feels a part of the family of God, gathered about the Lord's table. And the construction methods may well reflect those ancillary structures built to serve the neighborhood—the convenience grocery store, the service station, and the drive-in bank. Just because these structures are usually ugly is no reason to assume that they must be so. Indeed, the church could perform a social service by demonstrating that standardized building components can be used in creative and attractive ways.

III

Moving toward specifics, we notice a significant change in a third area, namely the *exterior profile* of new church buildings. The characteristic pacesetter church of the 1960s sported a high and dramatic roof line. Indeed, when one looks at the buildings most highly publicized through magazine articles and jury selections of the time, they almost look like a study in comparative roofs. By contrast, many of the most interesting churches built in the last few years have flat roofs and present a low profile.

The high and dramatic roof to the church of the 1960s is almost a trademark of that time. The A-frame and the parabolic curve were among the most noticeable. Uel Ramey's Holy Cross Lutheran Church in Wichita, Kansas, built in 1953, was surely one of the earliest of these, and their numbers multiplied throughout the sixties. Many other unique roof lines were explored, and the buildings of Victor Lundy became models of poetic hovering roofs. Frequently these dramatic roofs were combined with skylights or clerestory windows to create dramatic interior light effects, often focused on some spot, the altar or pulpit. Frequently the effect was that of baroque architecture, but it was combined with a technical virtuosity that baroque architects would have envied. We must acknowledge the creativity that often went into the design of those soaring roofs of the 1960s and the variety and beauty that frequently resulted.

But it is significant that during the late 1960s such forward-looking architects as Uel Ramey and Edward Sövik began building churches in which the roof was inconspicuous and the profile not particularly high. Such examples have proliferated in recent years.

Among the various emotive factors that people associate with the interior of a church, unusual height seems to be the most constant. One can get into quite an argument whether church interiors should be brightly colored or dark, well lighted or dim, rough-textured or smooth. People's power of association with what "looks like a church" will vary on these factors, but almost all seem to agree with the demand for unusual height. It is interesting that exceptional height should be the last of these emotive factors to be questioned. Of course, buildings with low exterior profiles may still give the illusion of excessive height on the inside by focusing light downward, and the shadowy criss-crossing of trusses overhead may suggest dark recesses that can pass for height.

Still, we cannot resist raising some theological questions. Is the move away from high profile buildings simply a matter of economics and new construction methods? Or is it a deeper move in worship away from a stress on God as transcendent to a recovery of the sense of his immanence? Certainly the economics of building today is tighter. But would we still want those tall structures even if we could afford them? The more restrained and modest buildings of our time show a move toward a *simplicity* that we previously failed to recognize as important. And it may reflect a deeper sense of the God who meets us in the midst of his people rather than up yonder in the distant haze. The flat-roof building may speak more eloquently of God than did the dramatic buildings of the previous decade.

IV

A fourth change, closely related to the exterior profile, has come about regarding the *interior orientation* of the building. The high roof lines of the 1960s usually focused attention on one spot in the interior, either by zooming downward dramatically or by soaring skyward spectacularly. The same purpose was accomplished by lighting too. But today's building is likely to be nondirectional. There is not likely to be any obvious "holy place" nor even a definite architectural focus. If there is to be such a place, it must be created for the occasion by the arrangement of the people and furnishings, rather than being predetermined by the architect.

I am not speaking especially of buildings designed to be multi-purpose which are often deliberately vague as to orientation and devoid of commitment to any special function. Such buildings have often, and with reason, been criticized as being good for everything and excellent for nothing. Spaces designed exclusively for worship use have also moved to a nondirectional approach.

Several factors are at work here. One of them is a deepened sense of the presence of Christ in the liturgical assembly itself and not just on the altar or in a tabernacle. The Quaker meetinghouse was often nondirectional in reflecting no concern with anything but the Spirit-filled congregation. Similarly, today's church may be more people-centered by making congregational space the only real liturgical space. Or it may be an unconscious recognition of the Spirit that blows where it wills! At any rate, separate and distinct chancels or sanctuaries, high and lifted up, seem to be increasingly relics of the past. The architectural features that tended to focus attention on such areas have been jettisoned in recent years.

Another reason for such change is that the liturgical uses of recent years are indeterminate themselves. We have recently passed beyond experimentation by incorporating it into our history so that innovation has become a standard part of worship for many congregations. This means that the interior ought to be indeterminate so that whatever needs to be done on each occasion can determine the arrangement and focus of the building, not unchanging steel and concrete.

Once one has such a space in which to plan worship, free and uncluttered by architectural focus, it is hard indeed to go back to a space where there is no freedom. And it is amazing how many imaginative possibilities in worship open up once one has nondirectional space. The most intriguing space I have ever worked in was an experimental theater where we were limited only by our own imagination. How hard it was to return from that to a directional church with a chancel!

We have discovered something we never knew before—the importance of *flexibility*. Why should a building be always the same for every occasion? Christmas is not Good Friday, a wedding is not a funeral, a Sunday morning congregation is not a Sunday evening assemblage. Yet we have often been content with a building that was always the same. Today, a wall is anything we want to project on it. Flexibility is vertical as well as horizontal. We built towers of steel scaffolding in our chapel once to convince students of that; our freedom is not limited to the arrangement of the floor alone.

I feel that the most satisfactory building shape for worship, as we know it now, is what I call a "hollow cube." I once convinced a student congregation to build such a worship space. I think they built it almost out of blind faith; now they can try experiments in worship that no other church in town can accommodate. "Hollow cube" may not be the best of terms, but it does express the basic sense of directionless space capable of a variety of orientations, of a level floor, of nothing nailed down or predetermined. In many cases, the vertical dimension may be less than the horizontal ones, certainly not greater than them.

A major change has occurred from the long history of church buildings with a very definite orientation around either a high altar or an equally high pulpit. We must remember, though, that until churches were filled up with pews, congregations remained mobile and essentially nondirectional. The nondirectional church building of today gives us both freedom and responsibility. For it is up to us to create the focus where it belongs for whatever occasion we are planning. The building interior, then, becomes a dynamic space where new centers of action can be created for whatever the occasion may be.

V

A fifth area of change is closely related, namely that of *seating*. We are finally realizing how much Christians lost when they sat down on the job in worship somewhere about the fourteenth century. The fluid and mobile congregation became an immobilized mass, wedged into a series of pews. And how we cherished those comfortable pews! I well remember the astonished disbelief I encountered when first I began questioning pews a dozen years ago, especially from one building committee that included a salesman from a pew company! Today, I suspect his firm also offers movable church seating; certainly its competitors do. A major breakthrough came when the St. Louis Episcopal Cathedral removed its pews in late 1969 or early 1970 and replaced them with movable seating. We could persuade people that if it could be done successfully in such a magnificent Gothic structure, certainly it could be done elsewhere.

One sometimes wonders: if we were really on our feet for worship (as Christians were for most of our history) would we need chairs at all? One solution in a California student congregation was a series of free-form risers in the floor with carpeted treads. These were relatively permanent but focused on no particular spot. Younger people often feel more comfortable sitting on the floor in their own proximities; I doubt you could sell that to older people who would just as soon be comfortable and keep their own distance.

The great advantage of movable seating, of course, is flexibility. One can shape the service around the people who are there, not around a mass of pews that may be unoccupied. A church with pews for two hundred is half empty when a hundred people show up. But the same congregation in a space set up with a hundred chairs will prompt the response that so many people have come that we may have to bring in extra chairs. Which is primary, the people who are there or the vacant furniture? Movable chairs put the focus first on actual people and second on the event. Perhaps the seating should focus on the font for some occasions, about a pulpit for others. We have these options and many more. With fixed seating we have no such choices.

Some manufacturers now make short, movable pews which

are attractive and heavy enough not to tip over. These may often be as satisfactory as and cheaper than movable chairs. Unfortunately, as soon as we mention movable seating, most people think of the cheap metal chairs on which they have suffered for years. Good movable seating is not cheap. But if it gives us several buildings instead of one frozen space, it may be the biggest bargain we can get. Such seating ought to be attractive, capable of ganging (linking), comfortable, and stackable (there are times when we will want to get rid of seating altogether). At any rate, movable seating is both a cause and a reflection of the changes we have seen in worship in recent years. Without it, many of our experiments would have been impossible; with it, we have attempted things we never could have dreamed of with a nailed-down congregation.

Yes, the church architecture of the 1970s is something quite different from that of the 1960s. But it will not stand still either. Those things that we find so true and obvious today will not all be so tomorrow. Anyone who builds today must shudder a bit at the danger of tying knots in the future. Certainly we cannot build with the bold confidence of those who built in the early 1960s. We have seen the middle ages in Roman Catholic worship end overnight and Protestant worship thaw almost as quickly, all within a decade. We know now how risky it is to assume that our needs for worship space will remain unchanging, so we have become much more reticent builders. Humility is not such a bad virtue in architecture or in life.

Perhaps change, then, is the greatest difference. Our church architecture has become open to change. Though it cannot guess the directions of future change, at least it has come to accept change as inevitable. And this is something that church architecture of past centuries never took seriously. This great openness to new possibilities is the major accomplishment of church architecture in our times. For this we should all be grateful.

Index